Praise for *Promotions Are So Yeste*

"Expand your horizons—and those of your employees! We know that 'promotions are so yesterday,' and yet we all fall in the trap of constantly confusing growth with positions. This book offers an updated road map for anyone who wants to develop themselves and their teams toward reaching their full career potential with tools and strategies within any leader's control."

—Ingrid Urman, Director, School of Management,
TenarisUniversity, Tenaris

"At a time when human connection is more critical than ever and harder to achieve, Julie has pulled together a practical field guide that busy managers can leverage to increase their teams' capabilities and personal career satisfaction, regardless of physical proximity."

—Heather Hoerdemann, Vice President, Team HR, and
Head of Talent, Synopsys

"This book is required reading for HR professionals and managers in every industry! *Promotions Are So Yesterday* offers a powerful and insightful new look at how leaders can approach career development in a way that inspires and motivates their employees."

—Marshall Goldsmith, *New York Times* #1 bestselling author,
Triggers, *Mojo*, and *What Got You Here Won't Get You There*

"Once again Julie brings amazing content for people managers who care about employee satisfaction and retention. *Promotions Are So Yesterday* empowers managers to adopt a new mindset around career development. Well-organized and to the point, the book also provides rich resources to support practical application."

—Marissol Mello Alves, PhD, Senior Program Manager,
Microsoft Career Development

"This book cracks the career development code for leaders and managers. By showing how to think outside the promotion box, Julie provides a plethora of practical possibilities for anyone who cares about development."

—Bev Kaye, Co-Author, *Up Is Not the Only Way*, *Help Them Grow or Watch Them Go*, and *Love 'Em or Lose 'Em*

"Julie uses employee insights and feedback to challenge people leaders and HR to reframe the why, what, and how of career development. She offers a playbook of research-backed tools that will help all leaders become better career coaches, developers, and facilitators."

—Mark Rhein, Director, Talent and Learning, Glaukos

"Julie has created a compelling story that resonates for leaders who want to create rock stars in the workplace by focusing on their most important responsibility—growing their team members. *Promotions Are So Yesterday* is not only a great read, it includes tools and strategies to support you in your journey of helping your team develop their best version of themselves, no matter what title they have."

—Allan J. Klassen, Chief Experience Officer, Brookfield Residential Properties

"If you're a manager who genuinely cares about helping your employees thrive, this is the book for you. With a keen understanding of how contemporary organizations really work, Julie Winkle Giulioni shows you the exact strategies you can use to engage and develop your team to the fullest."

—Dorie Clark, Author, *Reinventing You*; Executive Education Faculty, Duke University Fuqua School of Business

"Your employees may not want to 'play the game' or even 'climb the ladder,' but they don't want to get left behind either. What they want is a career to be proud of, one of contribution and fulfillment. This practical book will help you coach them to do that on their own terms."

—Michael Bungay Stanier, Bestselling Author, *The Coaching Habit*

"In *Promotions Are So Yesterday*, Julie captures the realities of today's workplace: Possibilities are the new promotion! This book is filled with tips, tricks, and tools for framing an engaging multidimensional approach to career development. The practical and example-based guidance for managers, who often dread career conversations, demystifies how to partner with employees to provide the development they crave."

—Melinda Kirk, General Counsel and Vice President of HR,
GDH Consulting

"If we don't make development our practice, then our employees will go to companies that do. Julie Winkle Giulioni gives you the canvas to make true development of your talent viable, applicable, and realistic. Grab this book and practice the C's with yourself and your people. You'll see the results!"

—Steve Browne, SHRM-SCP, Chief People Officer, LaRosa's;
Author, *HR on Purpose!!* and *HR Rising!!*

"In her remarkable new book, Julie Winkle Giulioni provides seven dimensions to help employees grow and find meaningful, rich, and varied experiences in their careers. For managers wishing to support growth aspirations of their teams, this book is a treasure chest of ideas to help employees see that career growth goes beyond the 'ladder.' I highly recommend this book and am keen to start introducing the seven dimensions at my company."

—Lucy Chaddha, Senior Director, TMP Innovation and
Learning, Salesforce

"*Promotions Are So Yesterday* offers sage advice that is spot on and to the point, especially in today's chaotic work environment. Promotions at work are certainly wonderful, but people hunger for so much more. Julie Winkle Giulioni has beautifully crafted a clear and practical approach to meeting this challenge in a way that engenders engagement, high performance, and retention. A worthy effort and a more worthy read."

—Doug Conant, Founder and CEO, ConantLeadership; Bestselling
Author, *The Blueprint*; Former CEO, Campbell Soup Company

"Consistent with Julie's gift for cutting through the chaos and offering reality-based solutions, this book offers a fresh and immediately actionable alternative to outdated ways of thinking about careers. Finally, a way to democratize development and empower a workforce capable of changing the world. Leaders who embrace this multidimensional approach to career development will enrich their organizations as well as the broader business community. Making change for good happens one person at a time, and *Promotions Are So Yesterday* offers the framework and resources to enable leaders to help everyone reach their greatest potential and thrive."

—Carrie Rich, CEO, The Global Good Fund

Julie Winkle Giulioni

Promotions Are **SO** Yesterday

Redefine Career Development.
Help Employees Thrive.

atd PRESS
Alexandria, VA

ATD Press is an internationally renowned source of insightful and practical information
on talent development, training, and professional development.

ATD Press
1640 King Street
Alexandria, VA 22314 USA

Ordering information: Books published by ATD Press can be purchased by visiting ATD's
website at td.org/books or by calling 800.628.2783 or 703.683.8100.

Library of Congress Control Number: 2021948338

ISBN-10: 1-952157-73-0
ISBN-13: 978-1-952157-73-8
e-ISBN: 978-1-952157-74-5

ATD Press Editorial Staff
Director: Sarah Halgas
Manager: Melissa Jones
Content Manager, Career Development: Lisa Spinelli
Developmental Editor: Jack Harlow
Text Design: Shirley E.M. Raybuck
Cover Design: Rose Richey

Text Layout: Kathleen Dyson
Graphic Design: LaRay Gates, Gates Graphics
Author Photo: Jamie Nease Portraits

Printed by Data Reproductions Corporation, Auburn Hills, MI

To Diane, Tim, Beverly, Bob, and Jackie—
my early managers who introduced me to the power
of development and possibilities beyond promotions.

Contents

Introduction:
It's Time for Moving Up
to Move Over

Is there anything more personal and rewarding than delving into someone's hopes, wishes, motivations, and dreams? Or helping them translate their priorities and goals into actions they'll take to create a new future? What's more familiar and potentially impactful than raising the mirror and helping people see the good, the bad, and the ugly? Or holding employees accountable for the development that they've indicated is important to them?

That's what career development is—and that's why it is one of the most intimate and important relationships you as a manager have with employees today. It's a profound and vital connection that has the power to forge unbeatable trust and loyalty, along with deep levels of personal and professional satisfaction in the workplace.

Done well, it makes a positive difference and leaves an indelible mark on others, as expressed by these employees:

"The time I spend with Minal around my development is the best part of my week. She listens. She hears me. She sees me. She knows me. And she challenges me to always bring more of myself to the table." —Data Analyst

"I've been offered other roles and even more money. But as long as Tim remains my boss, I'm not going anywhere. No one has ever been as invested in my career as he has." —Nurse

"I wouldn't be where I am—or who I am—if Karen hadn't seen something in me that I couldn't see for myself."
—Marketing Director

Too frequently, though, it's not done well. Stories like those of Minal, Tim, and Karen are overshadowed by the experiences of disenchanted and dissatisfied employees. And that's because in many organizations, career development is simply not working—or not working as well as it needs to.

The fundamental problem is that career development operates today as it has for decades. Businesses have evolved in nearly every other dimension of organizational life—from how they recruit, hire, and onboard, to the benefits and perks that are offered, to feedback and evaluation systems, to how, where, and even when the work gets done. But meaningful advances to career development have lagged, perpetuating outdated expectations as well as employee frustration, disengagement, and dissatisfaction.

And managers like you have been left holding the bag, blamed for not delivering the opportunities, possibilities, and growth that employees desire. The truth is that most of the dysfunction that exists around career development today isn't the result of your dereliction of managerial duties; rather, it's most often the result of deeply entrenched structural and mindset disconnects. Fortunately, you have the power to overcome these obstacles.

The Need for Change

The lack of progress and continued reliance on old approaches represents a significant liability because of career development's outsized influence on individual performance and organizational results. In fact, career development, growth, and learning are among the top reasons employees accept, remain in, or leave a role, and research bears this out:

- ▶ "Room for growth" is one of five keys to employee commitment and retention, according to the Hay Group.[1]
- ▶ LinkedIn's study of more than 6,600 working professionals found that 94 percent of employees would stay longer at an organization if they believed an investment was being made in their development.[2]

- 70 percent of US employees report being at least somewhat likely to leave their current employer for another with a reputation for investing in employee learning and development, according to a Harris Poll study.[3]

Retaining top talent—regardless of the employment market—is an increasingly critical priority, but it's just a drop in the ocean of benefits that effective career development can deliver. If as a manager you'd like to elevate engagement, unlock discretionary effort, inspire greater job satisfaction, or improve performance with your employees, career development is the strategy for you.

> **Career development is like a Swiss Army knife. It's one tool or action that delivers countless business (and human) outcomes.**

To employees, career development is no longer a nice-to-have, an extra, or something managers can do when they have the time. A workplace priorities, beliefs, and practices survey I conducted with nearly 800 professionals backs this up: 69 percent believed that one of a manager's fundamental roles is to support their employees' career development; this held true for everyone from young millennials to baby boomers.[4] Employees perceive career development as a core job expectation of their bosses, and one that too many managers are not able to meet.

Antiquated Approaches Can't Keep Pace With Contemporary Conditions

Just to be clear: Most managers want to offer the career development their employees crave. Most of you put tremendous thought, time, and effort into it. But today's landscape is congested with questions, contradictions, and complexities that leave too many managers fundamentally confused about how to best help others grow.

I'll bet you've struggled with at least a couple of these questions:

- How can people grow when promotions and moves are so limited?

- What kind of development commitment can employees reasonably expect when they will change jobs 12 times over the course of their lives and tenures average just over four years?
- How can we balance the needs that employees have to grow with the need the business has to perform?
- Where and when is development possible in light of fast-growing workloads and fast-shrinking discretionary time and budgets?
- How can growth scale—or even happen—given today's highly distributed and remote workforce?

These are confounding questions. And you need answers so you can deliver on the promise of career development for employees as well as the organization. So, whether you formally supervise the performance and development of others or are informally responsible for helping others grow through project management, coaching, or mentorship, this book is designed to offer you answers and, in the process, enable you to deliver greater engagement, satisfaction, and results.

Beyond, Between, and Besides Promotions

If you take nothing else from this book, I hope it's this: The time-honored tradition of defining career development in terms of promotions, moves, or title changes is dead.

Positions historically were the currency of growth and advancement. But this approach is no longer valid, for many reasons. The typical hierarchical pyramid narrows and limits opportunities to move up. There has been a thinning among the ranks of midlevel managers, leaving fewer levels to which to ascend. Fundamental changes have altered the workplace and how work gets done. People are living longer, working longer, and occupying boxes on the org chart for longer. In most organizations, there are simply not enough new positions to accommodate everyone who might want traditional growth. No wonder so many employees believe that career development isn't happening.

For too long, careers have been measured against major markers, points in time, and the artificial yardstick of new positions or titles. Managers—frequently with little control over promotional decisions—do what they can to help prepare others for new roles, but in many cases feel as powerless as their employees. The problem has been that we've focused so much attention on promotions that we've failed to recognize that careers are actually made up of many—often less auspicious or flashy—moments.

> **Beyond, between, and besides the upward climb toward promotions and positions, there are many other ways that employees want to grow.**

Contemporary development is a journey that evolves through countless (frequently small) moments that come together over time to create rich and multidimensional careers—and rich and multidimensional human beings. Just as life should be lived daily, by enjoying the journey versus myopically obsessing over the destination, so should careers.

This means expanding the definition of *career* to include all that can be developed and grown throughout one's life at work. And many factors are conspiring to make right now the ideal time for this to happen:

- ▶ The global coronavirus pandemic and everything surrounding it inspired a reassessment of lives, priorities, and goals. Long-endured trade-offs came into clear focus for many employees. For example, when parents began working from home, they realized how much of their young children's development they'd been missing. A greater focus on health and balance replaced hard-charging habits for many as they clarified what was most important to them.
- ▶ Old strategies associated with concentrating development efforts on high potentials have given way to more generous practices that make growth more broadly accessible. And today's increasingly virtual workplace has further democratized career development as organizations work to consciously level the playing field associated with growth, development, and advancement for all.
- ▶ Organizations have doubled down on innovation of their products, delivery platforms, processes, and more. This makes them well poised to advance an archaic system like career development as well.

An Invitation to a New Perspective

This is less of a book and more of an invitation. Each page will challenge you as a manager to evolve your assumptions about and approach to career development as you discover and learn to leverage seven alternative dimensions of growth that my research suggests are more interesting to employees than moving up. I invite you to explore a new language and expanded vocabulary around career development that inspires richer and more productive career conversations. If you decide to accept this invitation, you'll be rewarded with greater ease with and success from your development efforts—not to mention the fulfillment (and recognition) associated with leading teams of energized, engaged, and effective employees.

Chapter 1, "Promotions Are Overrated," will introduce you to a contemporary definition of career development and a framework designed to exponentially expand what's possible in terms of the growth of your employees. You'll get to complete a self-assessment that will illuminate new and potentially untapped sources of development for yourself. And you'll be introduced to a tool for helping employees accomplish the same thing.

Chapters 2 through 8 will delve into each of the dimensions of the framework: "Contribution," "Competence," "Connection," "Confidence," "Challenge," "Contentment," and "Choice." You'll consider the background research and rationale for each—but most important, actionable how-tos for supporting others' growth in new and different ways. These chapters are sequenced based upon the overall interest of the employees who participated in my research (which you'll learn more about in the next chapter). But read them in whatever order interests you. And use them as a resource when you're ready to help employees develop particular dimensions.

Chapter 9, "Possibilities Are the New Promotion," will pull it all together and offer some real-world tactics for dealing with employees who aren't quite ready to let go of promotions as their measure of success. Then, you'll be on your way with a plan to take action.

Because we all learn differently, this book offers a variety of ways for you to explore the ideas and strategies it contains. That's why you'll find:

- ▶ Straightforward descriptions of the dimensions—what they are, how they operate, and the opportunities they present
- ▶ Data and research that amplify and underscore key ideas
- ▶ Real-world examples of employee needs and how to meet them
- ▶ Streamlined recommendations for high-impact actions that translate each dimension into development
- ▶ Pro tips featuring targeted tactics that can take your efforts to the next level
- ▶ Checklists, discussion questions, tools, and templates to use with employees, all of which will make it easier for you—and them—to take action
- ▶ Additional content and perspectives in sidebars, which you can skip if you're tight on time and want to stick to the critical path
- ▶ Verbatim comments shared by employees who participated in my research study—and who capture the importance of these dimensions more eloquently than I ever could

As you read this book, you may find yourself wondering: "What about me?" Great question! You have a career to manage and develop too. And during the course of it, you've likely encountered the same struggle as your employees to find meaningful ways to grow beyond promotions, moves, and positions. So, rather than pushing it aside, lean into this question. Find ways to apply what you read to yourself. The more you use the ideas (with anyone, including yourself), the more fluent you'll become in new ways to approach career development. And that's good for everyone.

I'm excited to help you let go of yesterday's thinking and discover, embrace, and leverage today's definition of career development in the pages that follow. And I believe that you'll be excited too as you help employees grow in new ways over time—and as you experience the unbeatable satisfaction, potential, engagement, performance, and results that come with it.

1
Promotions Are Overrated

Three blind villagers heard about a curious new beast that had entered town and decided to go explore this animal, called an elephant. The first felt the tail and quickly pronounced, "Oh, I understand. This elephant is a rope." Another villager who had wrapped their arms around the animal's leg argued, "No, it cannot be. This elephant is a tree." And the final villager, with hands placed firmly on one of the elephant's ears declared, "You're both wrong. It's definitely a fan."

Don't worry. This book has not suddenly turned into a business parable. But if you'll indulge me, career development is a lot like the elephant, and we've all been behaving like those villagers, holding a small, incomplete view of it. The result? A microscopic understanding of what *career* encompasses. Self-imposed limitations on the possibilities associated with development. Daily missed opportunities to help others grow.

For decades, many of us have held firmly to one small part of this elephant that is career development. We've created and cemented our ideas about its totality based upon that incomplete experience. That's why promotions, positions, and mobility have been the face of career development for so long.

We've wrapped our arms around one part of the behemoth and have come to believe that career development is exclusively about the climb up and around the corporate structure. And because we've accepted this limited view of career development, we too are blind to the broader definition of the experience, the enormous possibilities that are present, and the many other ways you as a manager can help employees succeed and grow.

The climb—progression through promotions, positions, and moves—is how career development has traditionally been characterized and socialized in most organizations. With that as the default setting, is it any wonder that employees drink the Kool-Aid, adopt an upward orientation, believe that growing means going somewhere else, and establish expectations that can rarely be fully realized? No!

> **When climbing and moving are positioned as the only way to really develop, the message that employees get is "step up or stagnate."**

The result is we've inadvertently funneled people toward a ladder that can never accommodate them all—never mind that some of them don't want to climb anyway. This promotes competition, confusion, and frustration among employees that frequently fuel unwanted turnover for you and your organization.

But here's the good news. There's a whole new language available to managers who want to help others grow. The climb is only a small part of the career development elephant. In fact, there are seven other dimensions that can be developed throughout one's career. And when employees take off their blinders and become aware of the other viable and valuable ways they can grow, my research suggests that the climb suddenly becomes a lot less interesting.

The Backstory

When it comes to work, I've been fortunate. That good fortune is largely responsible for this framework and the additional seven dimensions of development you'll learn about in this book. I've been lucky enough throughout my career to work for one manager after another who just naturally knew how to develop people. For my first 15 working years, promotions were not a significant focus; in fact, the desire to move up only occasionally crept into my thinking. And that's because my career was full and fun and characterized by constant growth and engagement.

My first supervisor's default response was "yes" to the whackiest of challenges I came up with—even when I suggested bringing the circus to town (or our parking lot). He allowed me to dive into the deep end and intuitively knew when to let me flail around and when I was in over my head and needed a lifeline (or an elephant-sized pooper-scooper).

Another boss got to know me and my goals well enough that she knew to offer me opportunities to partner with our internal product development department so I could enhance my instructional design skills, which became the bread and butter of my career.

A university administrator to whom I reported appreciated my desire to contribute and make a difference during a particularly difficult period of change. She allowed me to assume responsibilities that were a bit out of reach—but that allowed me to have the impact I intended—and grow enormously in the process.

One manager sensed that I'd mastered my role and was running on autopilot. She facilitated the introductions necessary for me to support other regions within our organization and learn from their larger clients and more complex implementations.

These formative experiences as an employee painted a clear picture of how work can operate at its finest. These experiences taught me that careers are bigger than individual roles. That opportunities are constantly floating around waiting to be claimed. That growth happens in countless organic ways that have nothing to do with boxes on an organization chart or climbing the rungs of the corporate ladder.

Having managers who operated with an expansive definition of career development offered a visceral experience that's informed my point of view and my work as a leader, an author, and a consultant. I've spent years reflecting upon and dissecting those early experiences—and seeking out the stories of others who've enjoyed extraordinary development as well. The result is this framework, which breaks out of the old, limited career development box and creates the opportunity for more growth for more people more of the time.

The Multidimensional Career

As a manager, you have infinitely more ways to support employee growth when you help others develop a multidimensional view of their careers. The following self-assessment is designed to introduce you to the new language of development and orient you to seven additional development dimensions beyond promotions and positions. You can use this tool with your employees to help expand their thinking and jointly identify development priorities. (We'll delve into this in the following chapters.)

But for now, take off your manager hat and step into your role as an employee—the role in which you have your own career and would likely welcome growth. By completing the self-assessment for yourself, you'll:

- Become familiar with the dimensions.
- Gain insights into yourself and your own motivations.
- Have a sense of what your employees will experience if you choose to use this tool with them.

Your self-assessment results will reveal a landscape of dimensions in addition to and beyond the traditional focus on moving up or around the corporate ladder (which will be referred to as "climb"). These other seven dimensions are not only available for development but, according to my research, also deeply important and of genuine interest to your employees too.

TOOL The Multidimensional Career: A Self-Assessment

Circle the number in the table on the next page that best describes your level of interest in each of the following items. Then, transfer the numbers to the table below and add up the columns to arrive at totals for each development dimension. Higher numbers represent dimensions you might be most interested in developing. Lower numbers suggest less interest.

To What Extent Are You Interested In . . .	Less Interested				More Interested
1 Making significant contributions?	1	2	3	4	5
2 Learning as much as possible?	1	2	3	4	5
3 Cultivating relationships with others?	1	2	3	4	5

4	Building a sense of confidence in your abilities?	1	2	3	4	5
5	Stretching beyond your comfort zone?	1	2	3	4	5
6	Enjoying your work more?	1	2	3	4	5
7	Exercising greater control over how you do your work?	1	2	3	4	5
8	Getting promoted?	1	2	3	4	5
9	Making a difference and adding greater value?	1	2	3	4	5
10	Building specific skills or enhancing a talent?	1	2	3	4	5
11	Expanding your network?	1	2	3	4	5
12	Trusting your capacity to produce consistent, predictable results?	1	2	3	4	5
13	Exploring challenging experiences?	1	2	3	4	5
14	Feeling satisfied and fulfilled with your work?	1	2	3	4	5
15	Having more flexibility?	1	2	3	4	5
16	Changing roles or positions?	1	2	3	4	5
17	Aligning with your purpose for greater meaning at work?	1	2	3	4	5
18	Developing deeper expertise and effectiveness?	1	2	3	4	5
19	Creating a community of resources around you?	1	2	3	4	5
20	Feeling like "you've got this" in all aspects of your work?	1	2	3	4	5
21	Taking on or trying something entirely new?	1	2	3	4	5
22	Striking the appropriate work--life balance?	1	2	3	4	5
23	Exercising greater decision-making authority?	1	2	3	4	5
24	Securing a specific title?	1	2	3	4	5

1	2	3	4	5	6	7	8
9	10	11	12	13	14	15	16
17	18	19	20	21	22	23	24
Total _____	Total _____	Total _____	Total _____	Total _____	Total _____	Total _____	Total _____
Contribution	Competence	Connection	Confidence	Challenge	Contentment	Choice	Climb

And the Survey Says

In 2020, I conducted a research study of 750 working professionals aimed at evaluating the importance of, interest in, and access to alternative dimensions of development.[5] And the findings were nothing short of stunning. When respondents were made aware of alternative ways to grow beyond advancing through promotions and new positions (the climb), they expressed greater interest in every single other dimension overall. Here's how they ranked them:

1. **Contribution:** making a difference and aligning with your purpose
2. **Competence:** building critical capabilities, skills, and expertise
3. **Confidence:** trusting and appreciating your talents and abilities
4. **Connection:** cultivating relationships and deepening your network
5. **Challenge:** stretching beyond what's known and comfortable
6. **Contentment:** experiencing satisfaction, ease, and joy in your work
7. **Choice:** enhancing the control and autonomy you can exercise
8. **Climb:** advancing through promotions or new positions

With just one exception, regardless of age, gender, level in the organization, or location (the United States or elsewhere), employees expressed greater interest in all the alternative development dimensions. (Except for employees in their 20s, every other group we studied ranked the climb dead last. The 20-somethings ranked the climb second to last.)

These research findings should be welcome news for weary, wary managers everywhere. For years, conventional wisdom has instilled the belief that the bulk of employees are always angling for another role or to take the next step up the ladder. This kind of thinking has caused many managers to avoid career conversations altogether, assuming that they can't offer the growth their people want. Now we know that this is not true. Simply put, promotions are overrated.

For too long, the climb has been the celebrity of this reality show we call work. But the business landscape is changing, and my research offers insights into what employees want most.

It's time to counter the climb culture.

When it comes to helping others grow, managers have an entirely different language at their disposal beyond the traditional vernacular of promotions, positions, and moves—this offers countless alternatives to development that are not only more viable, but also more valuable to employees.

IS CLIMB LOSING ITS LUSTER?

Rising in the ranks and taking on higher and higher positions may not be as attractive to some as it was in the past. After all, the perks in many cases are not as great as they once were. Appropriately, the distinctions among levels are fading as status and compensation differentials are shrinking. Employees see firsthand the headaches and heartaches of managers who must constantly deliver exponentially more with infinitely less.

But it's not just what's happening in the workplace; it's what's happening outside as well, and new sensibilities are brewing. A growing movement toward authenticity is helping many people realize that the totality of *who they are* is not *what they do*. And this can inspire a long, hard look at the trade-offs as people work toward balancing, integrating, or harmonizing work and their broader lives.

These shifts in feelings toward growth through promotions offer you and other managers an opening to redefine career development and dramatically expand what's possible for those who are looking for a new relationship with their careers—and even those who aren't.

The Ultimate Win-Win

But employee sentiment isn't aligned exclusively around what interests people least. There is remarkable consistency around what interests them most as well.

When respondents were asked to rank the eight development dimensions, two rose to the top. Whether respondents were young or old, male or female, individual contributors or executives, located in the United States or elsewhere, they all expressed the greatest interest in developing contribution and competence. Although these two dimensions appear in different sequences for different groups, they remain in first or second place for every group in the study.

> **People *want* to grow precisely what**
> **organizations *need* them to grow.**

Employees actively want to enhance their capacity to contribute and their ability to perform. They are keenly interested in developing their skills and expertise. What organization wouldn't welcome that? What manager wouldn't celebrate it? Why have we been missing out on this opportunity for so long?

Employees across the board are interested in growing in ways that go far beyond the traditional definition of career development. And now is the time to help them make that happen.

HOLD GENERALITIES GENTLY

My research paints a compelling and consistent picture of how employees are most and least interested in developing. But keep in mind that each individual is unique. So, while you can use this data as a guidepost, it's important to avoid the temptation to pigeonhole people.

Understanding what's most interesting to each employee requires curiosity and a commitment to ongoing dialogue. Because what's interesting and important today will most certainly change over time. As one research subject shared: "What worked five years ago no longer fits my current stage of life. I like the flexibility of being able to continue to learn and grow but prioritize what matters most to me."

The only way that you will understand and be able to respond to changing stages of life—as well as to the kaleidoscope of other changes that employees experience—is through open lines of communication and frequent career conversations with others.

Relationship Reality Check

Helping employees embrace and act upon an expanded definition requires more than fluency with the language around these dimensions and creative ways to put them into practice. Career development, at its core, is a relationship. Until you've earned the right to be an active partner in someone's growth, techniques and approaches matter little. They're interpreted as another "flavor of the month," and your efforts can be discounted—or even worse, suspect.

Before considering how to apply these dimensions with someone, spend some time reflecting upon the nature of your relationship:

- ▶ What level of trust currently exists?
- ▶ What assumptions are you and this person bringing to your relationship?
- ▶ To what extent do you feel and visibly demonstrate benevolent concern for this person?
- ▶ What past experiences—good and bad—have defined or affected the relationship?
- ▶ How conscious are you of creating a psychologically safe environment?
- ▶ How might age, culture, education, experience, or other differences influence their level of receptivity to your involvement and ideas?
- ▶ How consistently have you supported and advocated for their development in the past?

The quality of the growth you can help others achieve is directly proportional to the quality of your relationship. And there are countless ways to enhance the quality of your relationships. Start by really getting to know others and their motivations beyond just who they are at work. Act in their best interest. Model vulnerability and authenticity so it's possible and comfortable for others to show up as their whole human selves. Foster a culture of psychological safety and inclusion to build and reinforce trust.

Your commitment to trust is central to building a relationship that supports meaningful development. Employees will open up about what matters to them and how they want to grow only in the presence of trust. They'll put themselves out there and into uncomfortable learning situations only in the presence of trust. They'll struggle, fail, and ask for help only in the presence of trust. They'll develop to their full potential only in the presence of trust.

So, how can you start? You already have a tool to launch the conversation—The Multidimensional Career: A Self-Assessment, on pages 4 and 5. Invite the employee to learn more about their career development priorities by completing a confidential self-assessment. You can use the clean copy of the instrument found at the end of this book. Better yet, direct them to the online self-assessment, which will automatically deliver a tailored report to the employee. This report goes beyond the paper-based version because it explains why "promotions are so yesterday," prioritizes the dimensions based upon responses, describes the dimensions, and offers reflection questions that will lead to a more thoughtful and productive conversation. (Information about this can also be found in the resources section.)

Once the employee has completed the self-assessment, schedule some time to discuss it. Allow them to take the lead, share whatever they feel comfortable disclosing from the assessment, and see where it goes. Whatever happens, you'll have established your sincere interest in the person's growth. You'll have introduced new language they can use to understand and express their interests, hopes, and aspirations differently. You'll be poised to deliver a personalized development experience. And you'll have taken an important step toward helping them enjoy a multidimensional career.

The Final Word

Opportunities to climb the corporate ladder and enjoy growth via promotions have become increasingly limited. Continuing to define careers and career development in these narrow terms will only perpetuate confusion, frustration, and competition. But there's an alternative to this outdated way of thinking—seven of them, in fact. They are contribution, competence, connection, confidence, challenge, contentment, and choice. And according to research, employees express greater interest in every single one of these alternatives than in the climb (growth through promotions and positions). This represents an enormous opportunity for managers who want to help their employees grow and thrive. And it paints a picture of a hopeful future filled with more development possibilities as careers become multidimensional.

"A successful career will no longer be about promotion."

Michael Martin Hammer, a former MIT professor and engineer

Expressed slightly differently, promotions are so yesterday. How can you prepare yourself and your employees to step into the future with new possibilities and an updated view of development?

2

Contribution

How can you help your people express their desire to make a difference—whether by doing more, adding value, taking greater ownership, being of service, or aligning with one's purpose for the satisfaction and growth it offers?

Nearly everyone wants to make a difference. We share a natural human drive to be of service. To help and support others. To offer our skills, knowledge, and experience. The desire to step out of oneself, be part of something bigger, and create meaning is an intrinsic motivator for many employees.

And, as the research I've conducted suggests, this need translates into a number 1 development priority and opportunity that managers can tap into. Of all the dimensions—contribution, competence, confidence, connection, challenge, contentment, choice, and even the climb—overall employees express the greatest interest in developing their contribution.

Many of those who participated in the research eloquently expressed their sentiments in comments like:

- ▶ "Doing meaningful work is paramount to me because I want to make my days here count."
- ▶ "If I'm not contributing to something bigger, I really have no interest in wasting my time."
- ▶ "We spend so much of our lives at work; it'd be an existential waste to have it deprived of meaning."
- ▶ "That's what life is about—making a contribution."

When employees are willing to bring a desire to contribute more to the workplace, everyone stands to benefit. After all, what manager in their right mind would reject more dedicated time and attention to the work, greater brainpower on tough problems, better ideas, higher productivity, or increased output from their employees?

"No thanks, I don't need people to step up more," said no manager ever.

At certain points in everyone's career, strategically tapping into what is possible and tuning into greater contribution can be the ideal vehicle for generating greater job satisfaction, renewed energy, and engagement. It's the ultimate win-win for the individual and the organization because, when approached thoughtfully and with intention, enhanced contribution simultaneously benefits both personal growth *and* organizational results. And you as a manager also win: As you build a team of employees willing to contribute and grow, you'll develop a reputation as someone who brings the best out in others.

Promotions, positions, and mobility—the traditional and outdated language of development—are generally dictated by organizational policies, and they're severely limited. But contribution, on the other hand, tends to be a broadly available option for focused growth. Think about it. Tapping into contribution is completely within your control as a manager, and within the control of your employees. It's not dependent on budgets, training schedules, or other frequently rationed resources.

This desire to contribute comes in all shapes and sizes and can play out in countless ways.

After years as a working mom, Heather has just sent her final child off to college and is looking to redirect some of the time and energy previously invested in family matters.

Naba is a recent college graduate who misses the activism and community involvement she engaged in on campus. Despite liking her work, there's just something missing.

At 65, Pedro scratches his head each time his boss brings up the topic of career development. He's simply enjoying what's likely his final act and just wants to make a difference and pass along what he's learned.

These employees are all—in their own way—perfectly poised to partner with their managers to leverage contribution as their next career development focus.

> **Strategic contribution is the ultimate win-win. It lets people *get* more development while *giving* more value.**

The generosity of spirit, the willingness to give without an expectation of anything beyond development in return, and the sincere desire to make a difference distinguishes individuals and builds careers. And yet, contribution as a development strategy operates at a subtler level than some of the other dimensions. For instance, it takes little effort to connect competence or challenge to career growth. That's a no-brainer. But contribution is less frequently discussed or positioned as a development strategy.

As a result, managers must invest conscious attention in educating employees about the potential of this dimension and in helping them intentionally cultivate contribution in a way that drives the growth they want.

This chapter highlights the role that dialogue plays, offering many questions you can ask to facilitate satisfying career conversations. You'll learn about five strategies you can use with employees (from newly hired to nearly retired) to amplify contribution and the growth it can inspire. And you'll consider how to keep this dimension, and the others, focused on development so that it doesn't become drudgery for your employees.

Dialogue Makes the Difference

Contribution happens day in and day out. That's how the world and organizations operate. And most people don't think too much about it. But routine, unconscious contributions—no matter how significant—tend to feel like just "work," meeting expectations, or doing the job.

For most employees, being mindful about how they choose to contribute isn't even on the radar screen. That's where managers come in. You can help elevate contribution so that it can become a career-driving focus through deliberate dialogue.

Jointly identifying contribution as the dimension to be developed is the first step. (The Multidimensional Career Self-Assessment takes some of the guesswork out by suggesting dimensions and priorities that others may want to pursue.)

Next, you'll want to guide employees toward formulating a clear-eyed understanding of what they might want to give and how to offer it strategically to support their growth. Not sure how to begin? Use the Questions to Clarify a Contribution Focus tool on the following page. Select one or more of the questions to incorporate into an upcoming one-on-one meeting. Consider sharing the question(s) in advance to ensure a more thoughtful dialogue. And allow enough time to really explore the ideas your employees raise. Beyond offering a rich opportunity to lay a solid foundation for meaningful growth, these questions also enable the kind of human connection and expression of genuine interest that build trusting relationships.

It's important to recognize that these questions, and the conversations that they inspire, go deep and will likely happen over time as trust builds. And you, as the manager, don't have to be the only one with whom the employee processes this information.

Adopt a "more the merrier" development mentality.

Employees need your involvement and support. But they'll also benefit from different perspectives. So, encourage people to expand and confirm their thoughts by exploring them with others in their inner circles. Family members, close friends, and trusted colleagues are in a good position to help clarify and refine how to leverage contribution for strategic development. And encouraging employees to take additional responsibility for these conversations and reflection helps them build the ownership required for sustainable career development.

TOOL Questions to Clarify a Contribution Focus

1. In what ways would you like to step up more or step up differently?

2. What more could you offer in your current role?

3. What's getting in the way of you bringing everything you've got to your work?

4. How might you find greater purpose and meaning in your work?

5. How might your work become more closely aligned with your personal purpose in life?

6. Which of your strengths and talents are yearning to be exercised more?

7. What difference do you want to make, or what value do you want to create, for others?

8. How might you be different because of the difference you'll make or value you'll create?

9. What would you like to achieve?

10. How will achieving this help you personally and professionally?

Once employees have begun to grapple with these questions (and the possibilities that their answers hold), it's time to explore specific strategies for leveraging contribution toward their growth and development. Here are several strategies to consider.

Connect the Dots

A critical step toward taking contribution to the next level is simply defining what it is today. In the rush of the day-to-day grind, it's easy for employees to lose track of how what they do supports the whole. In fact, a recent Robert Half Management Resources survey finds that fewer than half of those polled could make the connection between their day-to-day duties and organizational impact.[6]

This means that before people can start thinking about how they might contribute more, you must help them pause, step back, and define the importance of what they already do.

Connect the dots by asking your employees questions like:

- ▶ How does your work product support your team's results?
- ▶ How does that team contribute to departmental or divisional output?
- ▶ How does that output help the organization and its customers?

When you go through this kind of breadcrumb-trail exercise, you'll remind people of the significance of what they already offer, which helps to deepen a sense of meaning in their work. It can also illuminate those areas of a job where additional effort or attention might yield greater contribution to the organization—and to individual development.

Optimize the Current Role

Anyone's current role is a great starting point for considering how to expand contribution. It offers a juicy opportunity for greater contribution when looked at differently, when people ask themselves and others, "What are some opportunities for me to add greater value?" Because the truth is that any position can be more fully optimized by taking a critical look at what else is possible.

You, as a manager, are in the perfect position to tap into those possibilities by mining the mundane. You can help people see what they're doing every day through a different lens, one that picks up on otherwise invisible opportunities for greater contribution. This might look like challenging people by asking them to consider questions like these:

- ▶ What have you always wanted to do to better serve your customers?
- ▶ Which parts of the job description seem to routinely get short shrift?
- ▶ What tasks or activities need to be rethought or enhanced?
- ▶ Where could 10 percent more effort result in 20 percent more results?

This kind of reflection allows employees to look at their current jobs differently. It illuminates otherwise dark or forgotten corners of the role they already hold, discovering rich opportunities to contribute more and to grow more as well.

With the kids out of the house, Heather was ready to turn her attention to her development and maybe even position herself for additional challenges down the line. As a successful financial advisor, she consistently provided the responsive service her clients required. But she was ready to take things to the next level.

So, Heather met with her manager, Amina, and shared her desire to have a greater impact. They explored a few ideas for making that happen, and then Amina remembered a theme in many of their conversations over the years. She noted that on several occasions Heather had lamented the reactive scramble she frequently engaged in to respond to customers. They had always agreed that a more proactive communication cadence would be ideal—but Heather had never been able to do that.

Heather realized that the growth (and perhaps visibility) she needed would come from finally addressing this important dimension of her current role. Developing an outbound communication strategy was exactly the contribution she wanted to make. Together, she and Amina set goals, determined what resources were required, and crafted a plan that would allow Heather to begin authoring a regular newsletter and establishing a social media presence.

The months that followed involved a lot of trial and error. Amina was an invaluable sounding board, always asking great questions and helping Heather pause long enough to let what she was experiencing and learning sink in.

And it worked. Inbound calls went down, and client satisfaction went up. Before long, even the corporate marketing department was contacting her. Heather became a model for other advisors. Her business flourished, and she learned a lot as she elevated her contribution in her current role.

If we're being honest, very few of us have optimized our current roles. (I know I haven't.) There's always a way to offer more value. When people recognize this and when managers are willing to actively partner with them, employees will grow right along with their contributions.

PRO TIP

Prepare to run interference. Leveraging this dimension may require you to put extra effort into engineering an environment that enables optimal contribution. Sometimes that will mean neutralizing detractors, such as other employees who feel jealous or threatened as someone steps up and distinguishes themselves in new ways. You can do this by ensuring that everyone has an opportunity to grow in ways that are meaningful to them. Also, consider encouraging team members to openly share their development plans with one another and even offer mutual support.

But other things can get in the way too. Politics. Distractions. Barriers and roadblocks. As a manager, you're in the best position to partner with employees to both anticipate and address these obstacles. Brainstorm in advance what might get in the way and proactively identify strategies to implement should the need arise. Use your knowledge of the organization to help others navigate more easily. And when necessary, intervene directly to ensure that employees have the resources they need to contribute on a different or broader scale.

ADOPT A FACILITATION MINDSET

Fundamental to helping your employees grow is having the belief that people are smart, capable, and insightful. That they know what they need. That *they* are in the best possible position to make decisions about and for themselves when it comes to career development (and just about anything else.)

Managers who hold this belief tend to adopt a facilitation mindset. They understand that their value lies in helping others unlock and tap the deep reservoirs of knowledge within themselves to pursue contribution or any of the development dimensions. And they do this by offering the gentle structure and prompting that employees need to reflect, connect ideas and experiences, and arrive at their own choices.

This mindset plays out in any number of ways that profoundly affect the lives of those who are fortunate enough to work with a facilitative manager. If you'd like your employees to be among those lucky ones, consider trying on some of the signature mindset behaviors.

- **Exude curiosity.** Suspend judgment, set aside assumptions, and interrupt the habitual mind's distractions. Bring an authentic inquisitiveness to conversations—and relationships in general—to create space for others to contribute.
- **Ask questions.** Your employees generally have within themselves the answers, direction, or inspiration they need around important issues like development. Questions can be the perfect tool for excavating what's in there. Intentional, thought-provoking questions that help people think differently or more deeply facilitate insight and growth.
- **Listen intentionally.** For employees to arrive at their own ideas and conclusions, they need space to process their thoughts, talk through issues, and debate possibilities. Your listening allows for that space—especially when it's offered generously, leisurely (without pressing time constraints), and in an uninterrupted, undistracted way.

- **Promote accountability.** You can offer structure and be a champion, but others must be accountable to set their priorities, establish their intentions, and choose the steps that will help them succeed. Because if they don't take responsibility for all of that, there's a good chance they won't actually get around to taking action. So, combat any well-meaning tendency to be overly helpful and make sure ownership rests where it belongs—with employees.

When you reframe your role in terms of facilitating the insights, decisions, and ownership of others, the focus naturally shifts from you to them. And in that moment, everything changes. You send a signal of confidence that triggers the same in others. You inspire them to bring more of themselves to the conversation. You require them to be accountable. And you empower them to become the architects of the growth that they know deep down they want.

Adopt a Pet (Project)

Finding what employees are passionate about—opportunities to make a difference and have something tangible to show for their efforts—can elevate job satisfaction, engagement, and more. When strategically crafted, this is also an unbeatable strategy for career development.

Fortunately, in most organizations, there's no shortage of projects and initiatives that can offer meaty opportunities for greater contribution. Customer service initiatives. Cost reduction efforts. Technology migrations. Process improvement opportunities. Projects are plentiful—and are begging for people who want to contribute.

But what about when employees yearn to make a contribution that falls outside of business as usual, unrelated to the standard deliverables and operations? Sometimes people want to have an impact beyond the products, services, processes, markets, and customers. How can you help them satisfy that deeper need for meaning in a way that contributes to development?

Perhaps there's a mission-related department that needs attention. Or an initiative that aligns with an employee's personal values. Sustainability efforts, inclusion work, community outreach, and other social impact programs are always searching for passionate leadership and participation. So, work with your employee to seek out projects that make a difference and add value (to their development as well as to the organization).

> Naba, the newly minted systems engineer, discovered that although she had graduated from college, she hadn't graduated from her desire to make a difference. Her boss, Izzy, recognized this too. So, he initiated a conversation to explore what could be done.
>
> During the conversation, Naba candidly expressed her need for a greater sense of purpose. She also casually shared that she had been inspired to enter the field as a result of her experience with Girls Who Code, a nonprofit organization with the mission to support and increase the number of women in computer science. Izzy started connecting the dots, and pretty soon he and Naba were collaborating around the idea of their organization hosting a coding competition—which Naba would coordinate.
>
> Several weeks of approval gathering taught Naba firsthand how to navigate company politics. And several more weeks of planning and promotion helped to hone her logistical and communication skills. The event was wildly successful. The organization established goodwill and enhanced its reputation in the industry. And Naba's contribution benefited her in ways that will help her be successful with this organization and likely others in the future.

Naba developed herself while making a difference. And with some flexibility and creativity, your employees can develop their contribution and do the same.

Consciously and deliberately focusing on growing contribution is not something most employees (or managers for that matter) have much experience with. If it happens at all, it's generally by chance or a happy byproduct of another effort. But you can cultivate a more intentional approach with this Contribution Development Planner. Simply distribute it to employees and invite them to capture their initial thinking in draft notes that you'll review together. Use it as a basis for conversation, clarification, and contracting around what they'll do to leverage a project for the growth they want.

TOOL Contribution Development Planner

1. Describe the nature of the project. *This isn't a project plan as much as it is a narrative that captures the essence of the project and what it might offer.*

2. Specifically, how will you contribute to this project? *Focus on the signature strengths, talents, skills, and abilities you'll be able to deploy.*

3. Describe the difference that your involvement will make. *What will you bring to it that's unique, special, or important?*

4. How does this differ from your day-to-day contributions? *Being able to answer this is what distinguishes routine work from focused development.*

5. How will you feel once you've completed this project and made this contribution? *What experience do you intend to create for yourself?*

6. What might you learn and how might you grow through these contributions? *What else is in it for you and how will you be enriched as a result of this developmental experience?*

Make Extracurriculars Go the Extra Mile

No matter how hard you try, the workplace may simply not be able to meet all of an employee's developmental needs. But limited organizational opportunities and resources should never stymie people's ability to tap their desire to contribute and grow. Especially when the entire world can be their classroom. Savvy managers know how to capitalize on employees' extracurriculars. For instance, do they:

- ▶ Volunteer with a local charity?
- ▶ Help out in their kid's classroom?
- ▶ Sit on a nonprofit board?

I'll let you in on a little secret. To misquote a famous book title, "Nearly all I needed to know about leadership I learned when my kids started kindergarten"! Despite the countless workshops, assessments, and certifications I enjoyed, some of my most powerful leadership lessons came from volunteering at my children's schools: galvanizing people around a lofty goal. Wrangling volunteers. Making use of diverse skills and talents. Getting busy people so engaged that they'll excitedly invest those few off hours in the cause. Talk about transferable skills.

With some thought and intention, you can help employees leverage what they're already doing in their outside lives —not just to give back, but to take back to the workplace some valuable lessons and skills.

If someone is engaged in volunteerism, they're already contributing. So, work together to take a critical look at what they're currently doing outside work and see how they might squeeze more contribution (and development) value out of the experience. Is it time for them to step up to a leadership role? Take on a challenging project? Overhaul a system or streamline operations?

The key is to find the commonalities between work and life. Talk with employees about their extracurriculars and the growth they might offer. Create some synergy by linking (where appropriate) outside-of-work growth efforts to performance and development goals within the organization. If it's welcome, offer coaching and guidance, just as you would if the activities resided within the workplace. And recognize achievements, always highlighting transferable workplace applications.

An employee's ability to enjoy making a difference and developing themselves in the process isn't confined to the company's real estate or even to the hours they invest each day in work. So, encourage and support people as they look more broadly at the full range of opportunities in all parts of their lives.

PRO TIP

Recognize robustly. Don't hesitate to dole out praise generously when it's merited. While treating all employee fairly is nonnegotiable, that doesn't mean measuring out praise in equal portions for all. Extraordinary contribution that also delivers development deserves extraordinary recognition. Drawing positive attention to employees who invest in their growth sends a message about what's important to you and may inspire others to make a similar investment.

Unleash a Legacy

Engaging in deliberate and intentional legacy planning offers a clear lens through which to see (and perhaps shift) how an employee can make an enduring contribution to the organization and those around them. But it doesn't have to be a one-way street. Ensure that the traffic (and the benefits) flow in both directions.

> **(P)retirement: The period leading up to retirement.**
> **A rich opportunity for reciprocal contribution.**

Although someone may be wrapping up their career, more satisfaction, engagement, and learning are always possible.

As Pedro started to eye retirement, his focus naturally shifted. He and his director, PJ, became increasingly aware of the value of the institutional knowledge he'd gained over the years. As a result of ongoing conversation, PJ recognized that Pedro was very motivated to pass this along to others, and that finding a way to do this would satisfy his desire to make a lasting contribution.

So, they went to work on a plan that would allow Pedro to focus on knowledge transfer by creating a series of workshops and short instructional videos. But the benefits of this contribution flowed in both directions. PJ knew that Pedro was considering part-time teaching at the local community college after retirement. And this assignment offered him the opportunity to further develop his instructional and coaching skills, confirming his interest in this type of work and offering valuable and transferable skills that ended up serving him well.

This work tapped into his natural teaching ability and the pleasure he finds in coaching, mentoring, and sharing his methods with younger workers. And this might be a great opportunity to develop these skills and perhaps even explore part-time teaching after his departure.

Career development takes on a different complexion during different seasons of life. Late-career employees like Pedro have a lot to give to the organization. But don't count them out of the development game. There's still plenty for them to learn, and contribution is a powerful vehicle for facilitating that learning.

(P)retirement is a pivotal time for managers, employees, and the organization. You can help facilitate this transition in a way that allows for optimal contribution and growth through dialogue, using questions like these:

- ▶ What do you want to leave behind?
- ▶ What do you want to take with you (in terms of achievements, points of pride, experiences, insights, skills, or abilities)?
- ▶ What steps are possible to achieve both?

One participant in my research study shared a thought that has really stuck with me: "I believe that without contribution, we are never satisfied with our career." Enabling employees to find ways to enhance their impact, make a positive difference, live and work on purpose, and experience greater significance and meaning facilitates the career satisfaction and growth many are looking for today. And it positions these generous employees for the success they deserve in the future.

DON'T ALLOW DEVELOPMENT TO BECOME DRUDGERY

While these strategies offer the opportunity to tap into contribution for the purpose of development, they also come with a caution. It's easy for the additional time, effort, creativity, and resources that are being invested to become obscured. It's tempting for employees to get caught up in the excitement of offering more, and they might find themselves forgetting their primary intention. Before you know it, they're chasing additional contribution for contribution's sake, rather than for the sake of focused growth.

That's why it's essential when growing contribution—and all of the development dimensions—to work with employees to:

- **Set clear intentions.** Contribution can quickly become drudgery and just a lot more work unless it's grounded in the purpose of growth. Establish a goal and help employees to not forget the motivation behind their actions.

- **Extract lessons from experiences.** The activities that employees engage in open the door to development. But they won't walk through it and realize the full benefits until they pause and reflect. Bringing a curious mind to this extra effort offers the real opportunity for growth. What new insights are they gathering? Which skills are they strengthening? What are they learning about themselves, others, or the organization? Which efforts are delivering the best results? Questions like these (and the discipline you bring to asking them) will ensure that employees gain as much as they give.

- **Share what they learn.** To magnify the development that's possible through contribution, employees need to engage with others. So, encourage them to pass along their insights to co-workers who might benefit from them and to share accomplishments with you. (Make sure they know it's not bragging, but rather "flagging," when people offer the information you need to know to support your efforts.) Communicating like this benefits others while enhancing the employee's focus and commitment to growing through intentional contribution.

The Final Word

Contribution is a natural human drive. So, it's no surprise that it's the top-ranking dimension in my research. When greater contribution is consciously leveraged for development, the organization and employee both come out ahead. And being able to facilitate growth like this lies well within your sphere of influence as a manager.

There are many ways to tap contribution for development: reminding people of the purpose beyond their paychecks, mining current roles for greater value, crafting custom projects that meet personal needs, drawing extra-curriculars into the coaching process, even helping those approaching the end of their careers to cement a legacy. The key to making any of these things happen is dialogue, intention, and ongoing attention to how people want to contribute and how that can bolster their growth.

"If you want to live a long life, focus on making contributions."

Hans Selye, 20th century endocrinologist

Contribution is key to developing better health. How can you help employees use it to develop healthy careers as well?

3

Competence

How can you help people intentionally develop the skills,
knowledge, and capabilities they need to enjoy greater effectiveness,
experiences, influence, and satisfaction today while ensuring
continued relevance tomorrow?

It's no news flash that organizations face unsustainable productivity and profit pressure, with the constant drive to do exponentially more with infinitely less. Or that new sources of competition emerge daily, forcing enterprises to engage in constant disruption and innovation. Or that expectations continue to grow along with the demands placed on overstretched employees.

You know it, and so do your organization's leaders. In fact, 74 percent of CEOs are concerned about whether their organizations have the necessary skills.[7] Employees know it too; 70 percent worry that they lack the skills needed for today (much less tomorrow).[8] And because 85 percent of the jobs we'll be doing in 2030 have not even been invented yet, the future and careers of many are highly uncertain.[9]

Consider these contrasting examples of two business development professionals who work for one of my clients, a multinational risk management firm:

Despite the digital transformation that the organization was undergoing, Dave made the choice to double-down on processes he'd honed over the years—processes that he believed leveraged the human connection that's vital in a sales relationship.

Deb, on the other hand, leaned into the technology, seeing it as an important career growth opportunity. She prioritized becoming fluent in and taking full advantage of the resources supplied by the organization. But she took it a couple of steps further. She conducted her own research, developed a deeper understanding of the psychology of connecting with clients virtually, and identified additional tools to facilitate communication.

Not surprisingly, Deb flourished. Her growing competence resulted in extraordinary sales and customer satisfaction scores. But the benefits extended far beyond a performance bump. She felt engaged and became a resource to others who were struggling to embrace the digital transformation. She was invited to participate in round tables and task forces, offering greater visibility. Her investment in building her competence allowed her to take on more complex accounts and negotiate the ability to work from home two days each week—two career goals she'd set for herself. And when she had the time, she helped Dave, whose performance and career had stalled by comparison.

No wonder so many employees are eager to develop greater competence. In my research, it ranked second of the eight development dimensions. Survey respondents shared comments that would bring a smile to any manager's face. Comments about how important it was for them to "be the best" at what they did. How they wanted to broaden and deepen their expertise to "help the organization and others." How learning and growing was fun and enhanced their engagement. How it contributed to a sense of self-worth and pride in their work.

Other research subjects recognized and verbalized more existential implications. One person expressed it simply yet profoundly in this caution:

> **"Always be learning as if your life
> depended on it, because it does."**

With relevance and survival at stake—for both organizations and individuals—many employees embrace the need to develop greater skills, knowledge, and capabilities.

But few can do this alone. So, this chapter prepares you to offer the guidance, encouragement, and support that employees who want to develop their careers through competence need—and that managers like you are uniquely positioned to provide. Get ready to explore how to help others select high-impact skills that they feel committed to pursuing, as well as a range of strategies that allow for organic, in-the-workflow learning that's completely within your control to implement.

Determine the Developmental Direction

I believe that the world of work represents the biggest classroom on the planet. As a result, there are likely as many ways to approach competence development as there are individual careers—from formal classes and education; to observation, coaching, and mentoring; to targeted experiences and challenges. That's the good news for you as a manager as you engage in career development conversations with your employees. (It's also the bad—or sometime overwhelming—news.)

This plethora of possibilities can leave people confused and unsure about how to sort through the options and move forward. Employees welcome (and need) a collaborator in this process. Someone who knows and cares about them. Someone who understands the bigger picture and the various ways they can fit into it. Someone who recognizes what's valued and needed within the organization. Someone who can brainstorm viable and available ways to pursue new skills and competencies.

That someone is you! Employees will always get further faster with you as a partner, supporting their efforts.

> **Think of your role as that of a "capabilities co-pilot," "knowledge navigator," or "skills Sherpa"—a knowledgeable guide who can help employees determine what they want to learn and the best route to get there.**

You can assume this role by asking your employees questions like these to guide and focus their thinking and, ultimately, their planning and action:

- ▶ What exactly are you interested in being able to do—better, differently, or more of?
- ▶ What situations or opportunities do you aspire to be ready to thrive in?
- ▶ What capacities, abilities, or skills will help you reach number 1 and number 2?
- ▶ What are you motivated to learn or improve?

These aren't easy questions to answer. And it's not uncommon for employees (and even you as a manager) to struggle to respond. Be patient. Allow them time. Encourage employees to think and talk about it with others. Come back to the questions and be a sounding board as others think out loud, working through the answers in their own minds.

And if employees (or you) feel stuck looking at a blank page, introduce the following helpful starter menu of high-impact, high-demand skills. Simply review the skills with your employee—or invite them to review it in advance of a conversation with you. (You both should feel free to add other relevant skills as appropriate.) Ask them to identify which might add greater interest, effectiveness, or satisfaction to their roles. Then, help them reduce the number down to just one or a manageable few.

TOOL Menu of High-Impact, High-Demand Skills

❏ Agility	❏ Financial acumen	❏ Organization
❏ Collaboration	❏ Giving and receiving	❏ Planning
❏ Communication	feedback	❏ Political savvy
❏ Conflict	❏ Goal setting	❏ Problem solving
❏ Creativity	❏ Inclusion	❏ Project management
❏ Critical thinking	❏ Influence	❏ Resilience
❏ Decision making	❏ Innovation	❏ Self-awareness
❏ Design thinking	❏ Leadership	❏ Stress management
❏ Digital fluency	❏ Learnership	❏ Teaming
❏ Emotional intelligence	❏ Listening	❏ Time management
❏ Execution	❏ Negotiation	❏ Other_____

While all or many of these skills may be interesting and valuable to employees, counsel them against taking on too much at once. As the manager, you understand their current workload, their capacity, and additional priorities that will be coming their way. Employees understand their stress tolerances, their outside commitments, and the personal energy they can bring to development. Together, you can calibrate expectations and scope in a way that balances business demands and development needs. One to three priorities will generally be plenty to help people grow. (And the checklist isn't going anywhere. Employees can come back and layer on additional skills over time.)

LEARNERSHIP: TODAY'S META-SKILL

Given that the only constant is change and that the complexity and ambiguity we face today will likely persist, one fundamental meta-skill or competency should be at the top of everyone's development plan: learnership.

As one research subject insightfully noted, "The most important skill in today's and tomorrow's world is the ability to learn fast."

Learnership is the 21st-century skill associated processing, adapting, and applying evolving knowledge at the speed of business. It's about cultivating the habits, disciplines, and cadence of continuous learning today in preparation for a more productive and successful tomorrow.

In many ways, learnership feels like it should be a natural extension of the years we all spent in school, but it's different. Rather than being driven by the externally imposed pressures and direction that focused us as young students, learnership is internally motivated. It's structured not by a teacher's or anyone else's curriculum, but by the individual's unique interests and appetites.

What can managers do to help employees cultivate greater learnership? Encourage people to follow their interests and inspiration. Reinforce curiosity. Celebrate mistakes that yielded lessons. Allow time for reflection. Start or end meetings with all team members sharing one thing they've learned. Model learnership yourself: transparently and generously share your learning journey, sources, struggles, and insights.

Pressure-Test for Passion

Let's face it: A clear focus on building competence is not enough to ensure success. Given competing demands and countless other pressures, if the employee isn't genuinely and intensely interested, this effort will fall by the wayside. Passion—around the skills and abilities to be developed and how they support a person's career growth—is essential to translating intentions into action.

So, make sure to pressure-test the employee's development priorities with a couple of challenging questions like these:

- ▶ What's behind your interest in enhancing your competence in this way?
- ▶ What's in it for you to engage in this type of growth?
- ▶ What do you hope to do with your new or expanded skills, knowledge, or capacity?

If employees are unable to answer these questions, or if their responses lack conviction, you're looking at a red flag. It may indicate that they haven't connected with the development focus on an emotional level or that they're not sufficiently certain of its value. Or it may indicate that the identified skill or ability doesn't deliver on what they care about most.

Recognizing this lack of passion offers you, as a manager, the opportunity to dig deeper and help the employee reflect upon their reactions and level of commitment. Maybe it's just not a good or appealing fit right now. No harm, no foul. And no reason to continue down that path. Instead, use this as a chance to step back and find a different competence-building focus that will generate the passion necessary to learn and grow.

Prioritize the Nearly Endless Possibilities

Passion without action, however, is of little value. You and the employee must jointly determine how to pursue the desired skills and abilities. And the options for doing so are nearly limitless. How can you sort through the vast menu of possibilities and settle on the approaches that best suit the individual and what they want to learn or enhance?

The Snapshot of Competence-Building Options Matrix Tool shows one way of organizing the many development options available.

All available learning and development vehicles fall somewhere within this matrix:

- The bottom half outlines ways people can seek out and take information in as they consume knowledge and experiences. These activities lend themselves to people who have limited baseline knowledge or experience and would benefit from absorbing content and insights offered by others.
- On the other hand, the top half relates to the kinds of activities that don't formally present content but rather offer opportunities to create or construct new insights and learning for oneself. These can be ideal for someone who has some knowledge or grounding and is ready to build upon that and create a new or deeper understanding.
- The right side offers developmental experiences that involve other people—those who are more social in nature and depend upon the give-and-take with others.
- What's on the left side tends to be ways to learn and grow in a more independent, self-driven fashion.

TOOL	Snapshot of Competence-Building Options Matrix

Constructing

Self-assessment and reflection	Networking
New assignment	Information interviews
Greater responsibility	Communities of practice
Novel task	Committee membership
Targeted challenge	Mastermind groups
New focus	Coaching
Stretch assignment	Mentoring
Special project	Knowledge sharing
Books	Classes
Articles/blogs	Workshops/webinars
Podcasts	MOOCs
Videos/TED Talks	Conferences
Websites	Summits
Newsletters	Feedback
Online learning	Cross-training
Apps	Job rotations

Consuming

Solitary ◄————————————————————► Social

This matrix offers a framework for you to organize and consider the ever-growing ways to help people learn and develop. But it's also a tool for driving conversation with employees to help them explore, prioritize, and ultimately plan how to grow their competence. Effective managers use the matrix as a jumping-off point to talk about an employee's interest in different approaches, to explore which strategies might be more or less effective at delivering development outcomes and, importantly, which options are even available to employees. And you can too with these suggestions:

- ▶ **Interest.** Start by sharing the matrix with your employee and offering it as a tool for considering the range of options available to build greater competence in the areas they've identified. Invite them to review the options, adding others that come to mind, and circle the ones that are most interesting to them. Because people must own their development, they need to have a hand in determining what it looks like. And if the approach doesn't resonate for the individual, there's a good chance that the learning simply won't happen.

- ▶ **Effectiveness.** How someone wants to approach development is interesting—but will it produce the intended results? Test employees' thinking by asking them to look at the options that interest them through the lens of what will be most helpful. Based upon current knowledge, will they benefit more from consuming content or actively engaging in constructing it? How have they learned and grown best in the past? To what extent does what they're looking to develop require conversation and engaging with others? Help them cull the interesting options with an eye toward which will be most effective in reaching their goals.

- ▶ **Availability.** The final filter is whether employees can access their preferred approach. Some of the options outlined in the matrix are limited. By budget. By class size. By level. By the schedules of others. By internal approvals. Confront this reality honestly and openly with employees. Explain which items may not be feasible. Don't throw the organization or others under the bus, but be vulnerable and share where the boundaries of your authority lie. That allows you to shift the focus toward the left side of the matrix and the options that rely less on resources and others outside your control, and more on what you and the employee can influence.

> **You and the employee are in control when you lean into your joint locus of control.**

As a manager, you'll want to help employees take advantage of all of the relevant formal programs, courses, and resources that your organization offers. But there are plenty of other informal ways to facilitate greater competence—ways that rely upon little more than the creativity and energy that you and the employee bring to the opportunity.

Development rarely needs to wait for scheduled events. There's nearly always a way to make it happen right now and right there on the job within the context of an employee's current role. Where there's a will (to grow), there's always a way.

Encourage Transforming While Performing

I know (or at least strongly suspect) what you're thinking right about now: "This all sounds good, but how can I add development to my employees' already completely overflowing plates?"

You're not alone in this concern. The research that my co-author, Beverly Kaye, and I conducted for my first book, *Help Them Grow or Watch Them Go*, found that "lack of time" is a manager's number 1 barrier to career development. Over the decade, I've polled thousands of leaders worldwide, during keynote presentations, workshops, and web events. Not a single group has responded without time as a top concern.

But it's not just managers. Employees are also profoundly busy with work and other responsibilities. They feel the time crunch as well.

Of course, the conundrum is clear. An employee's investment in greater competence ultimately frees up more time as it increases capacity and the ability to perform. Feeling overburdened and stretched could serve as a visceral reminder of the importance of development

Yet, philosophizing aside, the question of time for development persists.

> ## Your employees can't squeeze more hours out of the day for learning. But they can squeeze more learning from each of those hours.

Too frequently, we treat development like a guest—something extra that's invited in on occasion. No wonder it can feel like an imposition that we need to find time for. But there's a better way of approaching it—one that doesn't require you to make extra space at the table or pull out the fancy silverware.

For development to operate at the speed of business, it must operate within the workflow—woven into and around authentic tasks and genuine contributions. That's how employees can transform while they perform. Real work in real time!

Here are just a few examples of how an employee's desire to develop greater competence and authentic business needs can come together to offer powerful opportunities for in-role development.

Tamera, a corporate services specialist, is interested in deepening her financial acumen.	+	Tamera's supervisor has some budgeting, forecasting, and analysis work that must be done.	=	Real-time, real-work competence-building experience for Tamera
Lucas, an assembly technician on the production line, wants to develop his leadership capacity.	+	Lucas's foreman needs someone to orient new employees to the team.	=	Real-time, real-work competence-building experience for Lucas
Antoinne craves broader exposure to the organization and the big picture.	+	Antoinne's manager feels burdened by one too many cross-functional meetings and could use more time to focus on leadership priorities	=	Real-time, real-work competence-building experience for Antoinne

The calculus is clear. There are countless ways to make your employees' desire for greater competence intrinsic to their work. Invite the development right into their day jobs. (Because concurrent work and development is the kind of multitasking we want to encourage . . . right?)

> **The work becomes the development.**
> **The development becomes the work.**

Dumping, Delegating, or Developing?

As you become more comfortable using embedded activities to help others elevate competence, you'll find more and more opportunities to blend development and work. It's a pretty seductive strategy. In fact, it's so seductive that managers can quickly overuse and inadvertently misuse it. Got a job to get done? Assign it as development!

But the typical employee can spot extra work masquerading as another "growth opportunity" a mile away. How you delegate and contract around an opportunity ultimately determines whether it's genuine development or just lazy dumping. Create an alignment-check worksheet like the tool below with employees to ensure that the proposed work will deliver development as well.

TOOL **Alignment-Check Worksheet**

Step 1: Note the task or assignment being delegated:	
Step 2: Ask the employee, "What are your current goals related to building competence?" Capture responses below.	**Step 3:** Together consider, "What development opportunities are embedded in this assignment?" Capture ideas below.
Step 4: Together compare the two lists and consider how the development opportunities might help the employee realize their goals for greater competence. Highlight the connections and determine the extent to which the assignment will deliver development outcomes.	

Here's what it might look like in practice as Regina, a manager at a regional utility company, and Adam, a customer service technician, work through the worksheet.

Step 1: Note the task or assignment being delegated: *Become a part of an incident prep team*	
Step 2: Ask the employee, "What are your current goals related to building competence?" Capture responses below. • *Enhanced communication skills (especially when emotions/pressure are involved) to make me more effective in my current role and more prepared for other opportunities that might present themselves* • *Broader knowledge of the organization as a whole to better understand how all of the pieces fit together* • *Deeper technical expertise to have a better command of my job and have the satisfaction of being able to help customers troubleshoot issues more easily*	**Step 3:** Together consider, "What development opportunities are embedded in this assignment?" Capture ideas below. • *Meet weekly with a cross-functional team to prepare for disasters and outages* • *Develop processes and communication that can be implemented immediately in an emergency* • *Review alerts from local emergency preparation, law enforcement, and fire authorities and prepare summary reports for senior leadership* • *Conduct a safety audit of one subregion each month* • *Become CPR and first aid certified*

You can see from this quick analysis that the incident preparation team opportunity supports Adam's goals because:

▶ Working with colleagues from other functions will dramatically expand his understanding of the larger organization.

- Getting out of his own space and routinely visiting other facilities as part of the safety audits will allow Adam a much broader perspective of the organization.
- Cross-functional work (the different people and issues it involves) frequently helps to hone communication skills.
- The experience of proactively creating emergency communication might provide Adam with strategies to better anticipate and deal with his own tense, emotional customer situations.

This sort of analysis doesn't cost much in terms of time, but the benefits are priceless. When you help people connect an activity to the growth they want, their commitment and learning are amplified. You won't have to be the career cop any longer, because development is deeply embedded into your employees' hearts—and jobs.

PRO TIP

Repurpose the Alignment-Check Worksheet for day-to-day delegation. You don't have to reserve this tool exclusively for use when working with employees who want to develop their careers by developing competence. Creating this kind of line of sight during routine assignment conversations can add greater gravitas and significance to the task, resulting in increased commitment. It's also good practice for you!

Helping others enhance their competence may simultaneously be your most selfish and selfless act as a manager. It's selfless because you're enabling the development of portable skills that make your employees more marketable. (And yet, it's pretty hard to leave a manager who's so invested in your career.) And it's selfish because of the profound benefits that you and your organization can reap in terms of job satisfaction, engagement, performance, and results. However you choose to look at it, investing in the competence of others pays off.

SUPPORTING DEVELOPMENT: THERE'S NOT ONE RIGHT WAY

While *support* sounds soft and gentle, it can show up in varied and sometimes hard-edged ways. For instance, it could look like working together to establish development goals that are meaningful and inspiring to employees. Other times, it's reminding them of their intentions and the investment they're making in themselves—keeping their eyes on those goals and holding their feet to the fire.

Sometimes it looks like anticipating distractions, obstacles, and barriers to development and proactively brainstorming ways to remove them. Other times, it's letting employees struggle and reflect as they figure things out for themselves.

Sometimes it looks like collaborating to identify the resources needed and jointly planning how to acquire them. Other times, it's challenging others to make the most of what's currently available.

Sometimes it looks like finding evidence of people developing in the ways they had planned and recognizing the effort, progress, and results. Other times, it's offering observations and feedback to help employees get back on track toward their development goals.

Your support will show up differently based on the needs of the employee and the context, but three best practices always apply.

- **Allow time.** Growth is messy. It can frequently be a "two steps forward, one step back" sort of experience. And although learning while doing real work offers obvious efficiencies, buffers and cushions should be built in so development doesn't become overwhelmed by the day-to-day grind.
- **Debrief development.** Development represents an investment—of time, energy, and sometimes other resources. Optimizing the return on that investment happens through dialogue. Help people slow down enough to recognize their growth. To let insights and experiences sink and settle in. To label and claim new skills and abilities for themselves. Liberally invite a pause and ask, "So, what are you learning?"
- **Enable application.** Growing capabilities will stop growing if they aren't put into practice. So make sure there are plenty of opportunities for application. If necessary, work with employees to find or create a context for new skills and abilities to shine. If they don't use it, they're sure to lose it.

The Final Word

Focusing on competence is an intuitive way to support the growth of others. It's intuitive because competence is an established piece of the development puzzle, and employees and organizational leadership broadly acknowledge the need for lifelong learning as essential to career success. But in addition to being intuitive, it's ubiquitous. There is so much that can be learned and so many ways to approach it that employees need your help to navigate the plethora of possibilities. This chapter offers a list of high-impact, high-demand skills that you can use as a starting point, as well as a framework that organizes the range of learning options.

While it might be tempting to default to formal training programs to meet the competence-enhancing needs of employees, don't limit yourself. Building informal, organic learning right into the workflow offers you unlimited flexibility and offers others unlimited opportunities to transform while they perform.

"Every day, and in every way,
I am becoming better and better."

Émile Coué, French psychologist[10]

You've got employees who aspire to this. How can you make it easy for them to grow their competence?

4

Connection

*How can you enable people to take the steps necessary to expand and
deepen their social networks, build productive relationships, cultivate a
sense of community, or enjoy greater visibility?*

"It's not *what* you know, but *who* you know" has been a business truism for
decades. Relationships make the world go 'round. There are books, workshops,
and an entire consulting industry designed to help professionals create, expand,
mine, leverage, and monetize their networks for greater success.

Today, however, people are looking for something more when it comes
to cultivating social connections—more than slick networking techniques,
clever elevator pitches, or ways to memorize names. They're looking for
authentic, nourishing, supportive human connections. Many employees have
become painfully aware that something fundamental is missing—in their
lives and in their work. And they've prioritized cultivating a sense of connection to meet this need and develop their careers.

> **"Flourishing in your career depends as
> much on your relationships, both in and out of
> work, as it does on your job itself."[11]**

As an independent consultant and author, I understand all too well that
connection is the lifeblood of business. Even so, I find myself routinely suc-
cumbing to the ebbs and flows of connection in my work. When I'm engaged

in intense, long-term client projects or when I'm writing a book, I retreat. I isolate myself, hunkering down and throwing myself into the work and the creative process.

At some point, though, I begin to feel disconnected. Work seems flat and one-dimensional. It becomes clear that something is missing. And when this happens, I know that what I need—for the quality of my work, for my career, and for my soul—is a renewed focus on connecting with other human beings in meaningful ways.

Your employees experience this need too. Have you observed others:

- Struggling to get their legs under them when joining your organization or department?
- Getting inspired to educate themselves about diversity, become more inclusive, or learn to be a better ally?
- Feeling stuck or stagnant?
- Craving access to new ideas, fresh thinking, and different perspectives?
- Wanting more visibility—either seeing more of the organization or being seen more?
- Looking to advance a great idea or plan that requires broad-based support?
- Aspiring to become a formal or an informal opinion leader?
- Experiencing a change in their personal life that shifted some of their social needs toward work?
- Wanting to feel connected to something bigger?

These are all cues that connection might be an employee's best next career focus. Cultivating new or different relationships offers perspectives and insights not always available through other development dimensions. Tapping into or developing a community provides support to reach goals. Social networks activate visceral learning that can lead to accelerated growth. But despite the benefits, employees will likely need your support to recognize and realize the development opportunities that lie within connection.

This chapter will help you do just that. You'll consider a number of possible ways to help facilitate the growth and connection employees are looking for. Strategies for enabling structured development as well as greater visibility will be explored in detail. The chapter will wrap up with a simple framework for helping people enhance the quality of their relationships, which, after all, is at the heart of connection.

My research got to the heart of this topic as well. Connection ranked third (behind contribution and competence) in terms of respondents' desire to develop it. Those in the study who were most interested in connection described the personal fulfillment, purpose, and meaning that accompany this dimension. But they hinted at more altruistic motivations that benefit the organization as well in phrases like "be of greater service to others," "multiply my value to the lives (of others)," and "part of overall value generation." In addition, women report significantly higher levels of interest in cultivating connection than men do, and they perceive it as more possible to achieve in their organizations.

Appreciation for this dimension appears to differ based upon organizational level as well as gender. Executives, vice presidents, and directors express significantly more interest in connection than managers, supervisors, and individual contributors. And those outside the United States report that this dimension is significantly less interesting and available to them for development.

HARDWIRED TO CONNECT

According to the classic self-determination theory research conducted by psychologists Edward Deci and Richard Ryan, connection (or as they termed it, "relatedness") is one of three fundamental psychological needs that we possess.[12] At a deep human level, we all want and need meaningful relationships with others. And given the considerable percentage of our lives that we spend on the job, the workplace is a natural spot for this to play out.

Connections also represent a significant source of professional growth and career development. Much of what we learn, we learn through others. We begin our lives relying exclusively on those around us to teach us. And by the time we enter the workplace, social learning—learning from, through, and with others—makes a significant contribution to our effectiveness and success.

Sometimes it happens in overt, visible ways through coaching, apprenticeships, mentoring, or interviewing experts. But more frequently, it seeps in covertly while silently studying a role model, taking in and acting upon feedback, picking up on new approaches through casual conversations, or busting through assumptions and biases while working with diverse team members.

As a result, connection can—and perhaps should—become a priority focus many times over the course of a person's career. Managers who know how to translate this fundamental need into development opportunities and activities will help employees grow while building networks that strengthen culture, retention, and results.

Ponder the Possibilities Together

Connection is a big dimension, spanning everything from amorphous feelings of belonging and commitment to tangible relationships. While employees may have a sense that this is a development priority, they may struggle to put it into words and crystallize what they're looking for.

You can help. When you pick up on cues that connection offers an opportunity for growth, or when employees complete The Multidimensional Career Self-Assessment (described in the resources section at the end of the book) and identify connection as highly interesting, help them—and you—develop a better understanding of this dimension with questions like:

- ▶ What does connection mean to you?
- ▶ How might enhancing connection(s) within the organization support your career development?
- ▶ Which parts of the organization would you like to gain a deeper and more personal understanding of?
- ▶ Whom would you like to get to know—and what would you like to learn from them?
- ▶ Whom would you like to get to know—and what value could you bring to them?
- ▶ What goals do you have that can be met only through others?

Time and energy invested in exploring these questions can deepen the manager-employee relationship while putting a finer point on how this dimension might support development. And that clarity is the first step toward moving forward and facilitating connection.

If you're like many managers, however, you might find that you have a limited repertoire of connection strategies. Beyond making a few introductions, what else is there? Plenty! Use the Targeted Connection Plan Worksheet on the next page with employees to help expand your joint thinking and identify fresh, effective strategies to meet their goals.

This worksheet acts as both an orientation to and a vehicle for planning action to move connection goals forward. Simply review the options in the first column with the employee. Use the questions provided to identify what holds the most promise or sparks the greatest energy. Then, the remainder of the worksheet will help you guide employees through the thought process of whom they want to connect with, what steps will be required to make it happen, and how they'll evaluate the extent to which their efforts were successful.

Make sure when you're doing this to pass the pen to the employee and let them capture and own the plan. Maintain the role of facilitator throughout the process. Your job is to ask questions, inspire reflection, challenge thinking, advance ideas, offer support, and tap motivation. Nothing less—and definitely nothing more. Assuming excessive responsibility for the plan robs employees of the ownership required for any meaningful development.

Too much help is frequently not helpful at all.

PRO TIP

Make ride-alongs how you roll. Do what it takes to make it easy and natural for employees on your team to double up and do things together. Encourage shadowing one another, attending joint calls, and visiting clients together for the purpose of development. Remove unnecessary approvals. Set the expectation that this is how your group operates and proactively address barriers and receptivity issues that might arise. Enabling this kind of casual, employee-driven collaboration and mentoring offers powerful learning and organic ways to connect.

TOOL Targeted Connection Plan Worksheet

Possible Activity	Connection Focus	Action Steps	Success Measures
Introductions Who can facilitate a warm introduction to those with whom you wish to connect?			
Collaborative Effort What projects or activities might allow you to organically connect with others in the workflow?			
Shadowing Whom would you like to spend time with or observe in action?			
Internal Meetings What activities or events within the organization might address your connection needs?			
External Opportunities Which events, conferences, or activities outside the organization might be helpful?			
Group Membership Are there any specific groups (affinity groups, peer networks, trade associations) that might help you meet your connection goal?			
Securing a Mentor Whose guidance and support might you benefit from?			
Becoming a Mentor Who might benefit from your guidance and support?			
Special Projects What real work that needs to be done anyway might offer the connection you're looking for?			
Job Rotation or Temporary Reassignment How might a short-term assignment in another part of the organization (or even outside the organization) expand your network/connections?			
Other			

Combat "Free-Form Anxiety" With Structured Development Experiences

As natural as making a human connection ought to be, it simply doesn't operate that way for a lot of people. Particularly in remote workplaces where technology has become the default communication setting, opportunities for casual, impromptu interactions don't present themselves as frequently as in the past. But, even when they do, many people express discomfort and anxiety when trying to connect in unstructured, free-form settings.[13] (Think about your own experiences: If you find yourself skipping networking events or sneaking out of cocktail parties early, you know what I'm talking about—and what your employees might be feeling.)

Fortunately, there's an effective way you can provide the structure that your employees may need to develop connection—one that also contributes to organizational results. It's collaborative project work, with a connection-developing twist. Consider a few examples:

When launching a traditional team/group project, managers typically . . .		When developing connection becomes an additional outcome, managers should do all of that and . . .
Focus on a business issue or opportunity that will be addressed.	→	Focus on development needs that might be accommodated.
Consider the skills and abilities required to advance the issue.	→	Consider the specific connection-related development goals of possible team members.
Convene a team that will solve the problem.	→	Convene a team that will help members grow through the connections that are developed.
Offer feedback and coaching related to delivering business outcomes.	→	Offer feedback and coaching related to achieving developmental outcomes.
Hold people accountable for results.	→	Hold people accountable for growth.

Leveraging projects as connection-developing vehicles for individuals—or for entire teams—likely follows a familiar framework. If you're already delegating, developing clear goals, agreeing upon processes, and tracking progress and results, you're halfway there.

With some slight adjustments, you can build upon your current delegation and team- or project-launch practices, extending them to facilitate the development of connection as well. The trick is to give the development aspect of the work its due so the overt business outcomes don't eclipse it.

By creating this kind of joint focus on a task or project, managers offer employees a comfortable context within which to do the sometimes-challenging work of connecting with others. It provides the "excuse" for interactions and gives people something else to focus on while building trust, alliances, credibility, affection, and more.

Terrance is the perfect example of a manager who knows how to structure work that delivers growth and development simultaneously—particularly around connection.

For instance, when the organization unexpectedly lost its right to use a bit of intellectual property central its top-selling program, Terrance knew that this crisis required immediate attention. He convened a cross-functional team that would clarify all the activity streams required to pull the product from the market, determine how best to deal with current customers and in-process deals, and create a replacement—all immediately.

Rather than engaging in a knee-jerk reaction and reaching out to the usual suspects, Terrance paused and looked across his teams. He recognized the profound learning that was possible from being part of this high-profile pressure cooker of a project. He also recognized that this was an ideal opportunity for Jess, a senior customer service specialist who had recently expressed an interest in development with a focus on connection.

Jess was thrilled for the opportunity to leverage her customer service skills and knowledge while getting to meet and work closely with people at more senior levels of the organization. And instead of just sending her on her way, Terrance previewed the team members with Jess and guided her toward determining whom she might be most interested in networking with and getting to know while resolving the business problem.

Shortly after the project got under way, Terrance touched base with Jess. She excitedly reported back on the progress of the team and the specific contributions she was making. When she paused, he recognized her effort and asked, "But what about your development? Who are you connecting with? What are you learning?"

While he appreciated the progress being made from a business standpoint, Terrance wasn't going to let Jess off the hook regarding development. The next time they met (and every time thereafter), Jess was prepared with a balanced update that consistently took into consideration how she was growing.

Collaborating with others to achieve something important offers the opportunity for employees to create connections with individuals. But it forges another kind of connection as well: a connection to something bigger than ourselves. And that sense of purpose and meaning comes with a whole lot of additional motivational side effects.

REMOTE RELATIONS REIMAGINED

In the years leading up to March 2020, virtual work was an anomaly or exception coveted by many but reserved for relatively few. Organizations and managers couldn't imagine wide-scale remote operations . . . until they had to. And the weeks and months that followed sparked soul searching and radical new thinking.

While wanting to tap the power and possibilities associated with leaning into remote work, managers grappled with the implications for connection and career development. In response, many organizations have adopted a "virtual first" strategy to work, which Dropbox explains "will give us the best of remote and in-person work, balancing flexibility with human connection, and creating a more level playing field for everyone."[14]

And, under the heading "be careful what you ask for," many employees who previously aspired to working from home have come to appreciate the advantages of co-location. Despite finding ways to remain connected virtually, many crave the experience of in-person human contact.

Managers everywhere are in the challenging position of navigating this evolving terrain. Doing so effectively requires understanding the needs and preferences of everyone. Creating alignment between what employees and the organization want. Checking conscious and unconscious work location biases at the door. And keeping a vigilant eye on each person to ensure that their connections to you, one another, and the organization remain vibrant and can fuel development—no matter where their work actually occurs.

Enhance Visibility

Another way you can facilitate the connections employees are looking for is through visibility. Visibility operates a bit like a two-way mirror. It allows people to see more of the organization and to be seen—in many cases at the same time. It's another budget-neutral, effective way to support development and growth.

Could you offer employees the opportunity to:

- ❏ Attend an event? Leadership meetings, customer events, industry gatherings, and similar activities offer a venue for employees to get exposure to a broader slice of the business as well as to meet and get to know others who may be helpful for their work and careers.
- ❏ Showcase their talents? Use employees' skills or superpowers as an excuse to draw attention to them. This allows them to make a positive impression while also making a contribution.
- ❏ Represent the team? You inspire pride—and allow people to enhance their connection—when you allow an employee to represent you or the team with others. (And a lovely side benefit is that you have more time for other priorities.)
- ❏ Lead a meeting? There's no rule that says you, as the manager, must lead every meeting. Allowing employees to demonstrate their skills and leadership reflects well on you and them. It offers a new perspective and allows others to see them in a different light.
- ❏ Meet key leaders? For many employees, little is more exhilarating than rubbing shoulders with senior leaders. And there's plenty to learn from such interactions.

❑ Speak at a conference? Speaking opportunities are a valuable way to establish thought leadership, challenge employees' skills and abilities, and enhance their network of connections.

Implemented with intention, these sorts of activities expand your employees' perspectives with exposure to individuals and issues that weren't in their view before. They also allow people to shine, contribute, and enhance their reputations in different settings.

Consider two simple questions to get people talking about the kind of visibility that will support their connection goals:

▶ What do you want greater visibility to accomplish for you?

▶ Whom do you want greater visibility with?

These questions will help you and the employee focus on a goal and co-create a plan to reach it. Sometimes employees will feel fully prepared to begin executing the plan on their own. Other times, they'll benefit from a manager's partnership and support to set them up for success.

Diedre leads a pharmaceuticals marketing team charged with ensuring the successful adoption of new treatments. Marcus has been on the team for several years, mostly focused on social media. He's recently mentioned feeling a little isolated and siloed. He's concerned that he's becoming overlooked because of his remote working situation. Diedre and Marcus have agreed that focusing on enhancing connection may be exactly what's needed for his career right now.

They determined that having Marcus represent the team at the monthly product marketing council meeting would allow him to reconnect with the broader organization, get on the radar screen of those in other parts of the business, and gain visibility with senior leaders.

To ensure Marcus's success, Diedre first reached out to the leader of the council to introduce Marcus, establish his credentials and authority to make decisions for her team, and explained the development purpose of his involvement.

Then she spent some time orienting Marcus to the personalities in the group. She reviewed the upcoming meeting agenda and described the issues that may arise. She asked Marcus how he might respond and offered coaching and additional insights. Marcus expressed that he had a plan and felt ready for the meeting.

But the plan—and even the successful execution of it—isn't the end of the story. People must reflect on what they're taking away from the experience to ensure that they achieve the connection they're looking for. Two more questions can help make that happen:

- ▶ What did you learn (about the organization, others, yourself)?
- ▶ What valuable connections were made—and how will you advance them?

When Diedre connected with Marcus the morning after his first product marketing council meeting, he was still flying high. In fact, she didn't have to probe much at all because he had clearly been reflecting on the experience overnight. He shared how had he begun to expand his network and highlighted some of the specific individuals he would be following up with. Marcus also reported learning about a new clinical trial testing protocol. And he asked for Diedre's approval for him to say yes to an invitation to join a subcommittee that would allow him to showcase his social media skills with others in the organization. She happily approved and they developed a plan to connect before the next meeting.

Coach Others in the ART of Relationship Building

At its core, connection is about cultivating relationships. And unsurprisingly, many employees struggle in this arena, frequently mistaking transactions for real relationships. As a manager, one of the gifts you can give an employee is the support they require to build and sustain productive workplace relationships. It's a gift that keeps giving throughout their careers.

There are countless articles, resources, and books on this topic. Find some of your favorites and share them with employees. Talk about your experiences building strong, sustainable relationships. And make it a priority to coach others in the fine ART of relationships.

Connection building is more ART than science.

Most people report that their most meaningful connections are typically characterized by three qualities—authenticity, reciprocity, and trust:

- **Authenticity.** Showing up as one's true self is the foundation of sustainable relationships. Faking it or trying to be someone you're not is exhausting; it's also off-putting to others. So, help employees cultivate their authenticity. Make it safe for people to be themselves and encourage them to invite feedback from others. (Just asking for help demonstrates vulnerability, which opens the door for genuine connection.) Help employees understand that relationships thrive when they keep it real.

- **Reciprocity.** The best and longest-lasting relationships involve a sense of mutuality and a two-way flow of energy. This doesn't mean that for every favor received, one must be immediately returned. But over time, both people should experience value from the relationship. So, challenge employees to perform a mental audit, considering what they're giving versus getting from key colleagues and others in the workplace. Encourage them to find and mine their spirit of service and generosity to ensure that important relationships remain in balance.

- **Trust.** While authenticity and reciprocity contribute to trust, so does everything else we do—or don't do. How we listen to others, or don't. How we show up to support others, or don't. How we express ourselves honestly and candidly—even when it's hard—or don't. It all feeds into the trust that others experience with us. Help employees understand this reality. Point out behaviors that affect trust when you see them. Make trust an ongoing theme in individual conversations and even team meetings.

When employees express an interest in developing connection, don't assume they understand—and practice—these things. Have an overt conversation. Together consider what the qualities of effective relationships mean to them and which they may need to give more attention to. Start with questions like:

- What's your personal approach to building and sustaining relationships?
- How well has this approach served you?
- What do authenticity, reciprocity, and trust mean to you?

- ▸ How frequently and effectively do you believe you practice them in your relationships?
- ▸ How can I best support your relationship-building efforts?

Coaching employees and helping them understand the mechanics of establishing and maintaining fruitful relationships will ensure that their focus on connection isn't a short-term ploy but rather an effort that will yield long-term development and career results. And the good news about enhancing their ART appreciation is that these sensibilities and skills go home with people and can enrich relationships in all aspects of their lives.

Practice What You Preach

One of the ways to inspire ARTful relationships is by modeling what they look like for others. When employees have the experience of you as authentic, reciprocal, and trustworthy, they're better able to behave in similar ways.

These behaviors naturally will help you cultivate your own network. And as important as these connections are to you, your day-to-day work, social needs, and longer-term career development, they might be even more valuable to those around you. Your ability to make introductions and broker relationships depends upon you establishing and maintaining a vibrant, collaborative network of relationships yourself. This includes within the organization, but also outside. Don't forget the value of connecting with vendors, partners, suppliers, contractors, consultants, and customers alike. Intentionally look for intersecting interests, shared challenges, possible collaborations, and joint opportunities to build a network of bridges to benefit all those around you.

The reality is that many people struggle with the idea of networking, describing it as awkward and uncomfortable and something they try to avoid altogether. If you're among them, this could undermine success—yours and your employees'. So, consider this: Your efforts aren't about serving you; they're about serving others. Reframing it in these terms can help reluctant network builders get out of their heads and into the world where connections can be made.

As one research subject observed, "Relationships are the most important aspect of any career or business." For most of us, connection is at the core of who we are and what we do. Be prepared for it to be a recurring theme with employees—and a recurring opportunity for growth and development.

The Final Word

Relationships have always been central to career development and success, and they've only become more important to employees who want authentic and nourishing connections in the workplace. Connection offers new and different perspectives, support, opportunities to learn, and a sense of community. And the give-and-take nature of relationships means that these benefits flow in both directions, lifting everyone involved.

It's within every employee's control to cultivate this particular dimension, and yet, many will need your help to develop an intentional plan for making it happen. You can support their efforts in a variety of ways from simply making introductions to strategizing ways to gain greater visibility to orchestrate targeted experiences and projects. And when you offer coaching around relationship building—and model it yourself—you help people grow and thrive not just at work, but in their broader lives as well.

"No matter what accomplishments you make, somebody helped you."

Althea Gibson

Career success is rarely a solitary endeavor. Relationships drive meaningful and fulfilling growth. What can you do to help others connect with the power of connection?

5

Confidence

*How can you help people have a more consistent experience of
"I've got this" at work by cultivating a realistic understanding of and
authentic appreciation for where their abilities and limitations lie?*

Anyone who's ever experienced a dip in confidence (and really, who hasn't?) knows that this dimension can have a disproportionate effect on career development and satisfaction. Whereas competence and contribution are accompanied by the fanfare of new skills, enhanced results, and outward achievement, confidence (or, more frequently, the lack thereof) operates on a subtle level, frequently going unnoticed—except by those struggling with it.

I know this from personal experience. When my first book was published, I had every reason to feel confident. *Help Them Grow or Watch Them Go* had become a bestseller. The ideas were being well received by wide-ranging audiences. I was getting invitations to speak around the world. And my insecurity was off the Richter scale.

Maybe it was because things had transpired so quickly, and I hadn't had a chance to settle into my role as an author. Or because, even though I'd written and spoken for years, I was new to bringing my voice to the ideas rather than packaging content for others to use. Or because I was flying solo in most cases, without a trusted colleague to tell me the truth about my performance. Whatever the reasons, it drained some of the joy from the experience and threatened my ability to make the most of the opportunity before me.

Insufficient confidence imposes an invisible (and insidious) ceiling on success and satisfaction.

The Business Case for Building Confidence

I'm not unique. You likely have employees who could make more of the opportunities before them if they enjoyed greater confidence. And, as a manager, it's in your best interest to help them achieve this. Confidence is one of the most heavily researched development dimensions. It's been found to contribute to a range of outcomes that matter not only to employees, but to you and the organization as well. If you're looking for greater happiness, improved performance, reduced stress, and greater risk-taking in your employees, look no further.[15] Confidence can deliver it all.

But to be clear, this chapter isn't just about building up an insecure employee. It's about supporting those who understand and want to mine the connection between confidence and their career growth, satisfaction, and success. This might include people who:

▶ Want to be more authentic. The business landscape is increasingly hospitable to bringing one's humanity to the workplace. But being whole, real, and vulnerable requires confidence.

▶ Believe they're a fraud. This feeling can be sparked by something like not holding a particular certification, degree from an elite university, or other credential. Or, people may have a nagging case of imposter syndrome (which 70 percent of us experience at some point in our careers) that causes them to attribute past success to factors outside their control and experience anxiety about "pulling it off again."[16]

▶ Skipped some steps along the way. This happens in many of the start-up clients I work with and other organizations experiencing hyper-growth. People rise through the ranks swiftly and become aware of some legitimate missing pieces or experiences that leave them feeling a bit less confident and complete.

▶ Are prone to perfectionism. Excessively high standards, unrealistic expectations, and destructive levels of drive frequently mask a lack of confidence. These behaviors, if left unchecked, can lead to burnout as well as mental and physical health challenges.

▶ Have learned a lot quickly and need to internalize and trust new abilities—like me and my new role as an author.

Confidence is the profound yet frequently overlooked dimension of development that boils down to trusting and appreciating one's talents and abilities. It's based upon an abiding belief that when capacity and effort conspire, results will follow. And it's important to a significant portion of the workforce.

Confidence ranked in the top 50 percent of dimensions that employees are most interested in. Those who responded to the survey described the pain of its absence. They also expressed the excitement, flexibility, influence, and ability to enjoy risk taking when confidence levels run high. One person summarized the thoughts of many by simply writing:

Confidence is the key to success.

This chapter outlines how to help your employees develop that confidence and the success it can bring. After looking at the unique psychological safety needs associated with this dimension, you'll become aware of the value of mastering tasks, discovering limits, and leveraging success for learning. You'll also consider four roles you, as a manager, can play as you champion the confidence-building efforts of employees.

THE GENDER QUESTION

Any contemporary discussion of confidence would be incomplete without at least considering gender differences. There are countless books, articles, podcasts, TED Talks, and studies on the subject. Sources ranging from Hewlett-Packard to the National Bureau of Economic Research to LinkedIn all point to a well-documented confidence gap.[17] Net-net: Women tend to evaluate their performance less favorably than men, be less inclined toward self-promotion, and believe they must possess 100 percent of what's required for a job before applying (as opposed to the average man's 60 percent threshold).

Yet, Jack Zenger and Joseph Folkman offer a more nuanced assessment.[18] They found that the greatest gap in confidence between men and women exists for people under 25. By the age of 40, the ratings come together, and after age 60, women's confidence levels actually overtake that of their male counterparts.

Despite perceived deficits related to confidence, however, my research actually highlights potential advantages for women relative to this dimension. Women are significantly more interested in developing their confidence. They're also more inclined to seek out connection, which can become a source of confidence. Finally, women see confidence as significantly more possible to develop in their current roles than men do. This combination of appetite and the perception of availability offers a potentially powerful coaching opportunity for managers— and growth opportunity for those who lean into it.

Dichotomy? Duality? Or Just Difficult to Discern?

Inspiring people to concurrently hold a clear-eyed assessment of today's capacity and an intention to push past these limits and continue to grow is just the beginning of the complexity associated with helping them develop confidence. At every turn, you'll find seemingly contradictory approaches. In the training I conduct, managers frequently ask, to help others grow confidence:

- ▸ Should I build someone up by focusing on what's working or what's lacking?
- ▸ Do I focus on successes or setbacks?
- ▸ Is it better to offer opportunities that reinforce strengths or stretch into the unknown?

To all, the answer is yes! Confidence is built and strengthened in a variety of ways. Sometimes through activities that yield confirming results and leave people with the deep knowledge that they've "got this." Sometimes through experiences that deliver disappointing news or redirecting feedback. But always with a focus on learning that will deepen self-awareness and contribute to a greater sense of clarity and assurance for the employee.

Swap Out Shame With Safety

There seems to be an unspoken and long-standing workplace rule around appearing self-assured and concealing insecurities from nine to five (or whatever your business hours might be). We've all heard—and likely spoken—well-meaning words that reinforce it. *Just suck it up. Fake it 'til you make it. Don't let 'em see you sweat.*

As a result, for many people, anything short of 100 percent confidence inspires a sense of shame. So, before you can even begin working with employees on this particular dimension, you must help them reframe the issue and shed the emotional baggage surrounding it.

Destigmatizing the desire to develop greater confidence is as easy as authentically sharing your own struggles. Relay stories of times when your confidence was compromised. Offer insight into the steps you took to move forward—what worked and what might have backfired. When executives, managers, and mentors openly discuss their own issues and insecurities, it normalizes the natural ebb and flow that most professionals experience around confidence. Your willingness to be vulnerable and authentic can inspire employees to shed the shame and demonstrate vulnerability and authenticity themselves, opening the door to deeper relationships and powerful growth.

Once safety replaces shame, you can get on with supporting others as they take steps to develop greater confidence, which, as one respondent to the survey put it, "comes from knowing exactly what you can and can't do." As a manager, you're well-positioned to help people realistically appreciate their strengths, as well as their weaknesses and the edges of their capacity today.

It would be easy to mischaracterize this sentiment as encouraging people to think small or stay inside the box. But when employees understand where the boundaries actually lie, it reduces ambiguity and anxiety. It unleashes energy and creativity that can be productively deployed within that space. And it allows people to act with confidence, knowing they can count on themselves and their abilities to achieve predictable results.

Locating limits is liberating.

Helping people understand and trust their current capacities and limits goes hand in hand with embedding the belief that they'll also be able to continue to challenge boundaries and expand what they're able to do in the future. And if you're thinking that this might not always be easy, you're right! (Hence the advice in this chapter.)

Hone What's Known

One of the most obvious yet overlooked strategies for enhancing confidence is to simply reinforce success around current skills or tasks. By consciously cultivating the experience of effectiveness around what they're currently doing, you can help employees internalize greater certainty around their capacity and knowledge. This elevates their trust in their own ability to perform predictably.

While not always the most glamorous or exciting vehicle for growth, repeating a task or activity can hone your employees' capabilities and create that sense of assurance, fluency, and next-level mastery that inspires greater confidence. But this doesn't occur as a result of mindless repetition. If that were the case, a lot more of us would have high degrees of confidence.

What's required is conscious, intentional practice—as well as guidance and support from a manager like you who is committed to enhancing confidence.

Kai manages a team of recruiters. Leland has been a solid performer for nearly two years until recently, when a few high-profile setbacks have seemed to leave him a little tentative and unsure of himself. Conversations between Kai and Leland uncovered that Leland's confidence had been shaken and that addressing this dimension was a priority for him and his career.

So, Kai did three things. First, Kai coached Leland to bring greater presence to his work by observing his conversations with candidates, noting the questions and strategies that surfaced great information—and those that didn't. Then, Kai touched base so that Leland could summarize his observations, what he did well, and what he could improve. At first, they met daily, then tapered off to weekly once Kai had the sense that Leland had formed the reflection habit. Finally, Kai invited Leland to share his recruiting best practices with a new team member. Within a few months, Leland's confidence wasn't just restored; it was boosted.

Leveraging current work toward greater confidence follows Kai's three-step process:

- ▶ **Presence.** Encourage employees to bring focused attention to what they do. They must observe their actions, behavior, or performance in the moment, noting what's working and what's not. This kind of mindfulness can be hard work—and sometimes feel like a whole other job layered upon the one they're already doing—but it will pay off in greater awareness, insight, and ultimately confidence.

- ▶ **Reflection.** These observations are important, but when they really start to address confidence is when they're cobbled together into insights. This requires employees to pause and think about it. Given the speed of business, you'll likely need to take the lead and carve out time for short conversations that allow employees to consider what they're learning and make meaning out of it. Otherwise, this step could easily get lost in the busyness that characterizes today's workplace.

- ▶ **Sharing.** Make sure that employees have adequate opportunities to share their insights. Putting people in a position to coach, train, or mentor a colleague requires the employee to think critically about what they know and do. This naturally generates a greater appreciation for one's skills and talents. Sharing knowledge with others also offers the opportunity for recognition and reinforcement from others.

With the appropriate structure and focus, you can turn any role into a rich source of insights about an employee's effectiveness, confirming competence and value and building the confidence they may be looking for.

Direct Them Toward the Discomfort Zone

Helping others grow confidence by delving deeply into what they're currently doing lies at one end of the continuum. But an equally valid approach exists at the other end, with a focus toward the great unknown instead. New, novel, or unfamiliar experiences also represent fertile soil for employees who want to plant the seeds of confidence.

When employees adopt the right mindset, stepping outside of what's known and predictable can make for powerful development. So, collaborate with employees to brainstorm possible projects, assignments, and tasks that represent a stretch using questions like these:

- ► What do you find difficult?
- ► What activities are you unsure you can successfully accomplish?
- ► What challenges or activities are uncomfortable?
- ► What experiences carry some risk and uncertainty?

Then, ask the employee to plot these possibilities out on a page that you draw to look like the Plot the Possibilities Tool.

TOOL Plot the Possibilities

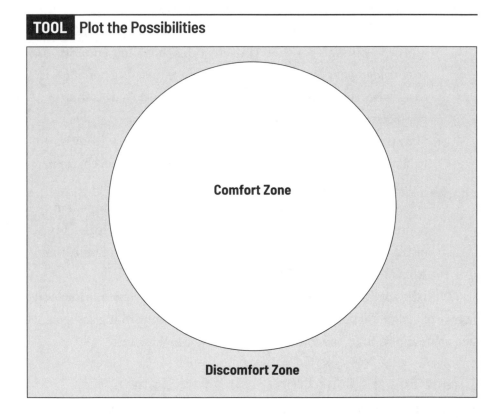

Invite your employee to orient each brainstormed idea in a way that demonstrates where it fits relative to the zones. Highly comfortable, no-brainer items should be placed toward the center of the circle; less uncomfortable ones will appear outside the circle; and wildly unsettling ideas that push someone's personal envelope should be captured toward the outer perimeter of the page.

Hunter, a project manager in the event-planning department of a large financial institution, knew he wanted to improve his confidence. So, his boss, Richonne, scheduled some time to "plot out the possibilities" using this tool.

Some activities Hunter could do in his sleep—things like creating the project plan and budgets for events. Those fell right at the center of the comfort zone circle and offered no development at all.

Other activities did not come as easily to Hunter. For instance, interacting with internal customers felt moderately challenging, primarily because the topic of conversation was generally deadlines they had missed. Hunter also experienced shaky confidence when speaking in front of large groups. Both were plotted toward the border between the comfort and discomfort zones.

And then there were the activities that fell well outside the circle, squarely in the discomfort zone. These included things like scoping new events and staying abreast of new technologies that could be used to track projects.

This simple snapshot allowed Richonne to facilitate a conversation about which activities made the most sense for Hunter to pursue to meet his confidence and career development goals. Together they confirmed that he loved being a project manager and wanted to feel masterful in that role (versus preparing for another position in the department). They also determined that "event season" (the busiest part of the year) was upon them and that he would have limited time and energy to invest in this development effort.

Hunter concluded that focusing attention on those activities so far outside of his comfort zone would ultimately be helpful to enhancing his confidence, but that he wasn't able to invest the energy required to take on something that challenging right now. He decided that while becoming a better public speaker would be nice in general, being able to better manage those internal conversations is what could really boost his overall confidence. So, Richonne and Hunter went to work on a plan to push the boundaries of his comfort a bit while honoring his current workload.

This simple exercise allows employees to consider and calibrate each possible activity so you have a basis for jointly determining that Goldilocks level of appropriate, tolerable, and confidence-building discomfort. It also offers you, as the manager, insight and ideas for ongoing coaching, recognition, and strategic delegation to support future growth.

Championing Confidence: The Four Roles

Elevating confidence doesn't always require formal development activities or tasks. Sometimes what's needed is a champion for the employee's success. And who better than you, their manager, to play that role?

Before you sign up, though, you should probably know that this role may differ from your classic, run-of-the-mill coaching. In fact, it's made up of multiple roles you can assume to help those looking to develop their confidence. At points in time, your employees might need you to be a confidence whisperer, truth teller, practice partner, or cheerleader.

CONFIDENCE WHISPERER   TRUTH TELLER   PRACTICE PARTNER   CHEERLEADER

Confidence Whisperer: Facilitating Ongoing Focus, Reflection, and Conversation

This role draws upon questioning and listening skills to inspire contemplation and conversation designed to develop an ever-deepening understanding of the issues and opportunities related to confidence. Depending on the situation, consider prompting reflection or dialogue with any of these questions:

- ▶ When have you felt your confidence soar? What specifically contributed to this? How can you tap into that again?
- ▶ What events or conditions in the past have triggered a lack of confidence?
- ▶ What's in it for you to focus on enhancing your confidence now?
- ▶ What would confidence look and feel like right now?

- ▶ What are you concerned about or afraid might happen in this situation?
- ▶ What's the worst-case scenario . . . and how likely is that outcome?
- ▶ What might this situation teach you—either through success or failure?
- ▶ What steps can you take to consciously leverage this opportunity toward a greater sense of confidence?

Truth Teller: Making a Commitment to 100% Honesty in Support of Development

It's not always easy to gain a clear sense of one's current capacity or contribution. And yet this is especially important for those who are working to develop confidence. Because they can't always trust their own (frequently negatively skewed) perspectives, these people need to know there's someone they can turn to who'll share the good, the bad, and the ugly.

If you really care, you'll give it to them straight.

Call it radical candor, the unvarnished truth, or just honest feedback—employees want and need it. When offered safely, with respect and genuine care, in the spirit of support, your commitment to sharing your consistently truthful perspective becomes an essential ingredient in building authentic confidence. For best results, consider these dos and don'ts.

Do . . .	Don't . . .
Make a clear agreement to ensure that the employee welcomes the truth.	Volunteer the unvarnished truth in the presence of others (unless it's positive).
Share your observations or direct information rather than judgments.	Sugar coat or soft-peddle the message.
Be specific and offer concrete examples whenever possible.	Make excuses on the employee's behalf.
Remind yourself and the employee that your goal is to enhance their clarity in support of greater confidence.	Respond in the moment if anything (distractions or emotions) might compromise the effectiveness of the communication.

Practice Partner: Acting as a Guide on the Side to Think and Talk Through Events and Opportunities

Think about the times you've walked into a situation knowing that you've got this. Did you anticipate what may transpire? Plot out possible pivots? Conduct a dry run? Verbally rehearse a range of responses? Preparation can contribute powerfully to confidence—yours and your employees'.

From time to time, having a partner who'll engage in these kinds of activities is exactly what an employee needs to work out the kinks, validate their ideas, and ultimately have an experience that moves them toward greater confidence. You can accommodate this by making yourself available to:

- ▶ **Be a sounding board.** "Talking it out" is an effective preparation strategy for many employees. They might already have a well-thought-through plan but would benefit from thinking out loud with you. Offering your ear—and sometimes little else—can allow others to recognize and challenge the wisdom of what they already had in mind.

- ▶ **Role play.** Many people appreciate the opportunity to practice in a safe environment before doing something for the first (or sometimes fifth) time. So, volunteer to play opposite your employees, taking on the role of others in an interaction and allowing them to try on new skills or approaches. To the greatest extent possible, behave as those involved might so the employee can experience a dose of reality. And offer feedback to reinforce what worked and alternatives for what didn't.

- ▶ **Engage in "what if?" questioning.** Overthinking is frequently the enemy of confidence. But you can disarm this dynamic by working with employees to talk through the possibilities and permutations in advance. Just getting the "What if?" questions out of their heads can be helpful, and the scenario planning that follows can significantly boost confidence.

Cheerleader: Cultivating More Positive Habits of Mind

One of the most harmful ways people undermine their self-confidence is through negative self-talk.[19] It's so easy to feed that downward spiral of self-doubt. And once you're sucked in, getting out can be challenging. That's where the manager as cheerleader comes in. From the sidelines, you're able to point out when your employee is engaging in this defeating habit and help them interrupt the cycle, generally with a dose of reality or an alternate positive perspective.

But don't stop there. Sustainable confidence depends upon employees being able to do this for themselves. Help people recognize signs of negative internal dialogue so they can interrupt it early. Encourage them to develop their own pep talks, even writing down key themes and phrases to remember. Over time, this positive habit of mind will not only allow employees to better manage their own confidence; it will likely have a positive effect in other aspects of their lives as well.

Learn From Successes

"Learn from your mistakes" is a familiar refrain because failure is positioned early and often as a powerful teacher. That's why most of us have become adept at recognizing our errors, reflecting on what went wrong and our role in it, and determining what we won't do again so we avoid future problems. We indeed do learn from our mistakes.

But can most people say the same about successes? When something goes well, do we invest the same evaluative energy? Do we conduct a robust after-action review to get to the bottom of what went right? Often, no. And it's an enormous missed development opportunity—perhaps especially for those who've recognized a need or desire to develop confidence.

So, flip the script and help your employees become as disciplined at wringing the same insight and growth out of their wins as they do from their losses. The next time something goes well, ask these three confidence-building questions:

> ▶ **What specifically did you do to contribute to the success?** Help
> people pause and recognize the connection between themselves,
> their efforts, and the positive outcome. Was it preparation? Special
> skills? Pulling together the right resources? (Don't let them off the
> hook with things like "good fortune" or "timing." These are not the
> kinds of responses that generate the deep sense of self-assurance
> you and they are looking for.)

- ▶ **What other conditions conspired to produce the success?** Nothing happens in a vacuum. The world is a kaleidoscope of circumstances—some that help, others that don't. Because it's important for people to experience a sense of agency and own their positive contribution, you definitely don't want them crediting things outside their control for their success. At the same time, confidence grows with a realistic appreciation for how other factors play into events.
- ▶ **What do you know now about yourself and your capacity as a result of this experience?** Positive experiences don't automatically translate into learning. So, create the space for people to crystallize their insights. Press for at least one thing they've learned—one thing that gives them greater confidence in themselves and their capacity to succeed again in the future.

PRO TIP

Encourage evidence collection. Because failures loom larger in our memories than do successes, invite others to keep a file (physical or digital) of compliments, achievements, and notes to look back upon as objective evidence of their effectiveness. You can also maintain your own collection for those working toward greater confidence. Periodically review with employees what you've collected on their behalf to offer irrefutable evidence of effectiveness and learning.

A Personal Postscript

Confidence is an invisible—but invaluable—quality, as anyone who's suffered its absence knows. Once I recognized my new-author insecurity for what it was, I was able to work on that dimension of myself and my career. I sought out others who'd traveled this path and solicited targeted advice. I invited feedback from a trusted mentor and worked with a coach who shared her sometimes harsh but always helpful assessment of my work. I learned to stop sloughing off compliments and instead take them in as important data points to be considered as well.

I'd be lying if I said that today I walk on a constant cloud of confidence. I don't. But the time I invested in this dimension boosted my sense of security and comfort in this role—at least enough to inspire me to write one more book.

The Final Word

Confidence contributes to career satisfaction and success. Sometimes developing it happens when employees discover that they can leap tall buildings. More frequently, it happens in less heroic ways—but only when managers work to create a safety environment. Helping others feel comfortable admitting to the need for or desire to enhance their confidence is an important and (sometime awkward) first step.

With that established, there are strategies that run the gamut—from drilling practices to the point that they become irrefutable strengths to actively seeking out the limits of one's capacity in an effort to define the space within which predictable performance is guaranteed. And when you support others through exercises like these by serving as a confidence whisperer, truth teller, practice partner, or cheerleader, you'll be championing the development of their confidence . . . and a lot more.

"Once we believe in ourselves, we can risk curiosity,
wonder, spontaneous delight, or any experience
that reveals the human spirit."

E.E. Cummings, Author

Confidence triggers a cascade of positive responses, relationships, and results. What are you willing to do to help others boost their belief in themselves—and give a boost to their career development as well?

6

Challenge

How can you help people step up, step out, and step into situations that
allow them to stretch beyond what's known and explore new, different,
and difficult experiences—all with a clear focus on development?

Take off your manager hat and think about your own career for a moment. What is the most profound professional development you've experienced? Where were you? What were you doing? What did you learn? And what was it about that set of circumstances that made the learning so effective? I'll bet it had something to do with a significant challenge that compelled you to draw upon your yet-to-be-discovered resourcefulness and skills to address a thorny issue or solve a significant problem.

In workshops, I frequently ask managers and executives about their most impactful development experiences. And one response that comes up time and again—from Lithuania to Los Angeles—is that someone threw them in the "deep end of the pool" and allowed them to figure out how to swim. It's the hard stuff that really tests abilities. The unknown that calls forth talents and gifts. The sometimes scary situations that tap inner resources. And that's why significant challenges are among the most powerful and memorable development activities that people engage in.

When the growing gets tough,
the tough get growing.

Challenges offer benefits on three different fronts:

- ▶ Employees enjoy the experience of stretch, skill building, and satisfaction. Challenges to perform beyond today's skills and abilities don't just combat boredom; they offer opportunities to learn a lot—and to learn it quickly.
- ▶ You as a manager benefit in terms of improved performance because your team will be able to accomplish far more as you blend growth with getting real work done.
- ▶ When challenges become part of a culture's approach to development, organizations have real information about a person's initiative, capacity, and progress. These actual experiences of employees stepping up can offer tangible input for better decision making around succession planning, for example.

In my research, employees ranked challenge fifth out of eight in terms of their interest. Those who prioritized this dimension were passionate about its ability to accelerate growth, unearth hidden talents, and promote improved performance. One respondent summarized the thoughts of many: "I believe that the most impactful learning and innovation happens when we go beyond our boundary and challenge our own limits."

In this chapter, you'll consider the mechanics of helping your employees do just that—from determining the optimal level of challenge, to specific tools designed to help you co-create experiences that transform meaty, meaningful, challenging work into powerful development.

Stretch But Don't Break

Challenging assignments (colloquially known by many as *development opportunities*, frequently surrounded by air quotes) are not a new idea. Some managers use them too much and often ineffectively—simply assigning more or harder work doesn't necessarily lead to the development, engagement, and satisfaction your employees are looking for.

This nuance was lost on me as a young manager. I had a talented analyst reporting to me—someone in whom I saw enormous potential. We had just won a large grant, and I offered her the growth challenge of developing the new tracking and reporting system. I knew she had it in her. I even told her so. And, remembering not to micromanage, I left her to her own devices. Much to my surprise and chagrin, it wasn't too long before she left *me* to *my* own devices. During the exit interview, she shared her experience of being stretched beyond what she was capable of and not having the support she needed to succeed.

> ## When a stretch goal is imposed
> ## by a manager, it's a mandate.
> ## When it's proposed by the employee,
> ## it's challenge-based development.

That was a huge wake-up call and profound learning experience for me as a new manager. In the years that followed, I discovered that finding the sweet spot where a developmental challenge taps the imagination, inspires effort, and optimizes growth—without overtaxing the human spirit—was possible. Finding that sweet spot is your job as a manager. The key ingredients are:

- ▶ **Dialogue.** Even your best managerial intentions aren't transmitted telepathically to your employees. Conversation is required. Sharing potential opportunities, hearing from employees, and collaborating on plans—this kind of dialogue makes development feel invited rather than imposed.

- ▶ **Purpose.** When you and the employee can describe and agree upon a specific growth focus, that transforms what would be perceived as "just more work" into targeted, electrifying development.

- ▶ **Skill level.** One of the primary reasons developmental challenges fail to deliver results is because the distance between where the employee is and what's expected is too great. A clear understanding of the starting point—in terms of skills, abilities, and even confidence—is the best first step in moving toward a desired future state.

- ▶ **Interest.** Motivation helps people weather difficulties because they know that learning is on the other side. Calibrating the employee's appetite for the challenge early on helps you determine what they'll be willing to invest.

- ▶ **Resources.** Successfully growing while performing one's job demands time and energy of employees. It may also demand resources from you and the organization. Failing to offer what's needed to produce the business results associated with the activity or assignment will nearly always compromise the learning results and your manager–employee relationships. Determine what's necessary for success. Is it budget? People? Time? Allocate resources as required.
- ▶ **Support.** In many cases, it's the priceless element of support from you, the manager, that's most critical for success. Your partnership acts as an insurance policy that the stretch will remain healthy and productive as you monitor progress, offer guidance, address obstacles, and suggest adjustments to ensure that the experience delivers the desired development.

Challenges and stretch assignments can be the perfect recipe for productive and cost-effective development—but only when you don't skip these important ingredients.

No Stretch of the Imagination

There is no limit to the possibilities that exist for facilitating development through challenges, because in most organizations, there's no limit to the challenges that face the business. Consider these broad categories as you and employees converse and collaborate to determine the specific set of experiences that will deliver the specific growth outcomes they're looking for.

Are employees interested in:

- ▶ Raising the bar by doing something better, faster, or cheaper for the customer? *Someone in manufacturing could stretch by challenging themselves to reduce production-cycle time.*
- ▶ Adding complexity to current tasks or roles (by doing it under more challenging conditions or with greater constraints)? *Someone who supports a domestic team could stretch by supporting international teams.*
- ▶ Increasing the level of responsibility (which could look like larger teams, bigger budgets, etc.)? *Someone responsible for sales to midsize companies could stretch by taking on a Fortune 100 account.*

- Finding a new context for existing skills? *Someone who facilitates customer focus groups could be ready to stretch by conduct a training needs assessment for the team.*
- Creating something new—perhaps a new product, service, or process? *Someone in software product development who sees an opportunity for wraparound consulting to support an upcoming launch could stretch by developing the service.*
- Venturing into voids by taking on ambiguous, ill-defined, or unclaimed projects or initiatives? *Someone in homebuilding who recognizes a recurring problem when customers take possession of their new homes could stretch by defining and documenting a more effective cross-functional handoff.*

These are just a few of the countless personalized possibilities for growth through challenge. And while each possibility will be unique, the general approach you'll take to helping employees think through, plan, execute, and learn from the challenges is relatively similar. The pages that follow explore specifically how you might facilitate two different scenarios from the beginning and end of the list: raising the bar and venturing into voids.

Raise the Bar

In many cases, you don't need to look any further than an existing role to find challenging ways to help others grow. In fact, it can be as simple as a deliberate effort to ramp up the volume, speed, or accuracy of the work in a way that benefits others and leads to greater or different results.

Eli, a software services manager for a hospital system, understands the importance of challenge better than most. She routinely helps team members step up to meaningful challenges that interest them. As a result, her group's performance, engagement, and retention results are enviable.

During a recent development conversation, Randy, an analyst who reports to Eli, expressed a desire to challenge himself a bit more in his current role. He'd seen some redundancies and inefficiencies in a particular process and believed he could write, test, and implement a level 1 alert in five weeks as opposed to the usual six or seven.

Eli was thrilled at the prospect of exploring this opportunity for growth, which would also improve departmental cycle times. At the same time, she understood that speeding up the process alone wouldn't necessarily result in the development Randy was looking for.

So, she worked deliberately with Randy to ensure a clear growth focus as he raised the bar on his performance. Together they personalized the experience to meet his unique needs by creating an accelerated project plan and identifying specifically what he was going to need to do differently to meet the milestones. He was going to have to begin interacting directly with the physician lead and updating the health records steering committee—neither of which he'd done in the past, and both of which represented significant growth opportunities.

Eli provided some background and perspective around working with the physician lead. She made an introduction to several members of the steering committee so that Randy could become acquainted with their expectations. She volunteered addition support as needs arose, making sure to remind him that the goal was not just to deliver the software more quickly, but to deliver his growth most effectively.

Here's the process that Eli followed—and that you can follow too.
- ▶ **Ensure that the purpose is developmental.** You and the employee need a clear agreement that this "bar-raising" experience is designed for growth first and performance second. Sure, you'll likely get more or better work done in the process, but keeping a clear focus on your joint intention to generate development throughout the experience will ensure that growth remains in the foreground.
- ▶ **Personalize the challenge to the individual.** Collaborate to establish new goals related to volume, pace, accuracy, or other relevant metrics that interest the employee. Remember that unlike performance expectations, these are self-driven objectives for the purpose of development and they're valid only if employees

genuinely desire and own them. So, let your employee take the lead to ensure a personalized plan, but feel free to offer your perspective. People need to hear if you think they can do more. Or if you're concerned that they're setting themselves up for something less than success. Or if you believe that these goals could endanger other important work. Offer your counsel but allow final decisions to rest with the employee.

▶ **Be the partner they need to succeed.** Development is a team sport, so ensure that employees aren't left to play entirely solo. Some will welcome frequent check-ins and the offer of support or resources. Others may want a wider berth to enjoy the struggle associated with self-sufficiency. But all want to know that they have the support of their manager as they work to raise the bar. So, contract for what they need. Discuss how they learn best—and how they want to learn during this experience. Ask what help looks like to them. Determine what level of support they'd welcome. And agree specifically upon how, when, and if you will intervene to ensure optimal development.

> **Greater velocity, volume, or accuracy isn't squeezing more work out of people. It's squeezing more development out of the work.**

PRO TIP

Don't let growth get lost in the grind. Be aware that what starts as a self-imposed challenge or improvement goal can quickly become tedious or overwhelming in the face of the day-to-day. Combat this reality by working with employees to maintain the necessary focus and energy. This may be as simple as reminding them of the development-related purpose behind the choice to raise the bar.

You might also find it helpful to work together to add some additional gratification to their growth. Consider how they might gamify the process. Or how tracking the headway they're making visually with charts and graphs might punctuate progress. Or how incremental celebration points could sustain effort over time. The key is to maintain momentum, so the challenge has a chance to deliver the desired development.

DYNAMIC DUOS, TREMENDOUS TRIOS, AND MORE

By now, you've likely noticed that the eight development dimensions rarely operate in isolation. Consciously developing by taking on a challenge, for instance, can at the same time:

- Enhance contribution as employees step up and take on greater responsibility.
- Build competence, because challenge is one of the forms of experience-based learning addressed earlier.
- Elevate and break through confidence boundaries.
- Introduce new connections as people take on assignments and activities that may involve others.
- Position someone for a move when, as, and if a climb opportunity becomes available.

As tidy as it would be for these dimensions to stay within clearly defined borders, that's just not how the world, or development, works. The lines are blurry, and thank goodness. Because when various dimensions converge, people enjoy more growth—more efficient growth—and more satisfaction as a result of growing in multiple ways.

When you appreciate the broader definition of development that the multidimensional career offers, you become well-poised to use the eight dimensions together synergistically to generate dynamic duos, tremendous trios, and any number of other combinations to facilitate powerful development outcomes for your employees.

Venture Into Voids

Voids are all too familiar in organizations. They are the "white space" between departments and teams. The overlapping functional boundaries where issues slip through the cracks. The pinch points in the customer's journey. The organizational or process issues that everybody recognizes but nobody owns. Whatever their nature or source, voids are among the most underused yet powerful types of challenges available for driving growth.

Voids are chock-full of opportunities for employees to make a real difference and to quickly acquire a range of new skills. And the amorphous and frequently interdepartmental nature of the challenges offer a rigorous informal course of study in complexity, collaboration, creativity, execution, and so much more.

What makes voids a potentially attractive strategy is that, like other developmental challenges, they meet a real need within the organization, yet, at the same time, the bar for success is relatively low. Because they represent problems that aren't being addressed anyway, even small strides in the right direction are deeply appreciated and disproportionately recognized. As a result, those who step into a void immediately distinguish themselves, garnering attention and visibility while gaining valuable lessons that could never be learned within the context of the daily grind.

Voids are one of Theo's favorite strategies for employees who want to use challenges for the purpose of development. Theo is a regional director for a landscaping firm. Lizel is one of the office associates who report to him. During a regular one-on-one, Lizel expressed interest in enhancing her influence and problem-solving skills. After some conversation, they determined that introducing a new challenge to her current role might be the best way forward.

Theo had been aware of a problem that had been brewing at several residential properties. Individual homeowners, the homeowner association, and property management company personnel had been experiencing persistent confusion over billing and scheduling for the past several months. This issue fell squarely at the intersection of multiple departments and groups, and it wasn't significant enough to hit anyone's radar screen yet. All of that made it the perfect void for Lizel to explore, experiment with, and use to expand her skills.

Lizel jumped at this opportunity. She and Theo worked together on a plan, ensuring that her influence and problem-solving focus would be front and center. She conducted interviews, reviewed the data, and convened a couple of meetings. And it wasn't long before she was zeroing in on the problem: The lines of communication among multiple sets of stakeholders were getting tangled and information wasn't getting to the people who needed it. Once the root cause was validated,

Lizel proposed developing a simple app and went to work to gain the required buy-in. By venturing into this void, Lizel was able to focus on and develop key skills of interest to her while delivering real value to the organization.

Powerful stuff, right? But people will rarely find their way toward these challenges without some insightful dialogue and skillful guidance from managers like Theo—and you.

The Taking On the Challenge of a Void: Planning Worksheet on the next page can serve as a framework for you to use with employees as you jointly consider and plan to venture into voids that might offer the challenges necessary to meet their specific development needs.

You might be wondering: Do I need to keep a constantly refreshed library of voids to offer employees? My answer is, "Not necessarily, although I'll bet you've already got one in draft in the back of your mind." These sorts of situations pop up constantly. Now that it's on your radar screen, you might recognize them more quickly for the development opportunities they offer.

At the same time, remember that employees must own their development. You're not exclusively responsible for creating the development context. So, brainstorm ideas in response to the first question about existing voids. If you and the employee can't come up with any viable ideas, invite them to go on an organizational scavenger hunt, looking for problems they can solve—and grow from. Ask around yourself. Imagine what a hero you'll be when one of your employees is willing to step up to a challenge identified by a colleague.

Once you've identified some solid ideas in response to the first question, work with the employee to complete the rest of the worksheet. While you may need to get involved when it comes to things like approvals (question 5) and resources (question 7), the employee should take the lead to the greatest extent possible. Because even before jumping into the void, there's growth to be found in planning for it.

TOOL Taking On the Challenge of a Void: Planning Worksheet

Questions to Consider

1. What voids exist?

2. Which of these voids interest or energize you?

3. What could you learn—or how could you grow and develop—by addressing the void?

4. What do you hope to contribute to the situation?

5. Whose approval is required to begin?

6. What's your plan for addressing the void? What steps will you take?

7. What resources will you need? (time, people, budget, facilities, equipment)

8. What challenges might you encounter?

9. What steps could you take to avoid or address these challenges?

10. How will you evaluate the success of your efforts?

Consider the broader ecosystem. Work with vendors, suppliers, and customers to explore ways to share resources informally to support development across your employee populations. Short rotations or joint projects offer unique challenges not possible internally, as well as an entirely new worldview for those involved.

Cross the Finish Line

Working with your employees to co-create the growth challenges they want and need requires an investment on everyone's part: time, conversation, creativity, energy, patience, follow-up. Yet all too frequently, that effort produces lackluster results. For many, it's because of confusion about where the finish line lies.

Once the challenge has been met, it's tempting to check off the experience as complete—to brush your hands together and think, "My work here is done." But nothing could be further from the truth.

> **Your work is *not* done until you've helped the employee illuminate the learning.**

The challenge itself remains in the realm of mere activity until or unless its implications and insights are considered and properly processed. Employees need to extract the lessons contained within the experience. That's what transforms challenges into meaningful and actionable development. This is the finish line that you must help employees cross. And until they do, they can't realize the greatest value and growth from your joint investment.

This kind of reflection doesn't always get its due given the frenetic pace of today's workplace. That's why it's critical for you to help others take the time to step back, ponder, internalize—to claim their learning—and to consciously decide how to leverage new insights, skills, and abilities. Simple, yet profound, questions can be asked throughout the process and at the conclusion of the developmental challenge. Questions like:

- What do you know now that you didn't know before?
- What can you do now that you couldn't do before?

- ▶ How can/will you apply new knowledge and skills?
- ▶ What's next?

Effective managers understand that helping others illuminate their learning is as important as—maybe even more important than—the time spent co-creating the challenge-based experiences in the first place. And they invest accordingly in the reflection and conversations that unlock the full benefits of the development effort.

Let's not overlook the importance of that final two-word question, "What's next?" Some employees will be ready to quickly take on the next challenge. In these cases, this question offers an opportunity to explore what that might look like as you begin the whole process all over again with the employee. But note that other employees may respond differently. They may be ready to prioritize another development dimension. Or they may have gotten more challenge than they bargained for and need a good, long break before scaling the next mountain.

Just as night follows day, recovery must follow experiences of challenge. While the time required to rest and recharge may differ among people, you should promote an appropriate pause to help prevent burnout, allow new skills to become part of the employee's internal operating system, and ensure sustainable interest in development. (This is where our next chapter on contentment will pick up.)

The Final Word

When employees add intensity, high stakes, or complexity to their work, they're setting themselves up for challenges—as well as for profound growth. Development accelerates in the presence of difficulties that stretch people beyond where they are today. But be careful of trying to pass off harder or more work as a "challenge"—because employees know that any old work doth not development make.

For a challenge to be developmental, it must be purposeful and consciously aligned with that employee's growth goals. Agreed upon, not assigned. Calibrated to an appropriate and healthy level of stretch. Supported through success and struggles. And thoughtfully processed each step of the way through ongoing dialogue that highlights the learning and growth that the challenge delivers. As this chapter showed, you play an invaluable role here.

"Challenges make you discover things about yourself that you never really knew."

Cicely Tyson, Actress

Want to tap unknown talents, surface hidden opportunities, and allow employees to step up in meaningful ways that deliver real value to the organization, their growth, and their careers? Challenge yourself to challenge others.

7

Contentment

*How can you help people find within their current situations or roles
the heightened sense of satisfaction, pleasure, and ease they may
need or desire? How can you help them prioritize enjoying the journey
of work over arriving at a particular career destination?*

I remember growing up and hearing from older family members, "It's called work for a reason; if it was enjoyable, they'd call it fun." It seemed a dark characterization—even to a child—yet it reflected a generation's experience and sensibilities about a job's role in our lives.

Fast-forward to the 21st century, and seismic shifts have occured in the nature of work and what employees now expect (dare I say *demand*) from the countless hours they invest in a job each week. The pendulum has swung for employees from just punching the clock and laboring joylessly through the day to wanting to actively enjoy and even have fun at work.

In fact, happiness has become a significant strategic focus for many organizations. Witness the introduction and rise of the C-level role of chief happiness officer or of Zoom's Happiness Crew and Google's Jolly Good Fellow.[20] Organizations have sought to elevate the employee experience with creature comforts like free food, Ping-Pong, and pool, plus other wellness benefits like gym memberships, nap pods, and unlimited vacation. Many organizations are making concerted efforts to cultivate cultures that offer a sense of pleasure and enjoyment to the experience of work with these sorts of extrinsic motivators. And some are seeing positive results—at the individual and enterprise level.

Even so, the half-life of these measures and the satisfaction they generate can be short. And they tend to inspire an upward spiral of expectations that, when not met, can cause employee engagement to nosedive. A more sustainable approach draws less upon organizational intervention and more on the manager's role in connecting authentically with employees and tapping into their intrinsic motivation.

Ping-Pong can't possibility compete with a genuine personal relationship and understanding of what matters to your employees. Nap pods become a big snoozer when compared with getting to know people and the broader context of their lives. And free food feels like empty calories when a manager's genuine commitment to personalized well-being is on the menu.

Contentment operates at a personal level and requires personal attention.

You—rather than the organization—have the greatest effect on employee contentment. Managers who recognize this opportunity (and privilege) will find themselves better able to activate contentment and support the broader career success of their employees.

The people who participated in my research study helped me better understand the nature of these internal needs. Those who were most interested in developing greater contentment expressed a deep desire to "enjoy the work" and "feel fulfilled and satisfied." They shared the importance of well-being, balance, health, and rest, which enabled them to enjoy their personal lives while sustaining the energy required for long-term career success. And they also spoke of engagement, excitement, joy, and effectiveness. This all leads to something deeper than the fleeting nature of happiness. I've chosen to use the term *contentment* to describe this more fundamental experience (and the development dimension that goes along with it).

Of course, I'm not the first to highlight the importance of these positive emotions. Volumes of research conducted on the subject make the case for contentment and its career-supporting benefits. Happiness and well-being:

- ▶ **Increase productivity.** Enhanced performance and effectiveness draw positive attention to an employee and can lead to greater opportunities, visibility, and career success.[21]
- ▶ **Boost creativity and innovation.** These are two high-impact skills that nearly everyone in the workplace needs—both to remain relevant as individuals and to contribute to the ongoing relevance of the organization.[22]
- ▶ **Result in greater initiative and fewer sick days.** What manager or organization wouldn't welcome this? The drive that distinguishes one employee over another is key to career development, satisfaction, and success. It's essential for business success as well.[23]
- ▶ **Make someone appear more likable and trustworthy.** Perceptions matter in the workplace. And those who are perceived to have these positive qualities typically enjoy more and better relationships. It frequently telegraphs leadership capability and enables the kind of growth discussed in chapter 4.[24]

Productivity, creativity, healthy, trust—all of this contributes directly to vibrant, successful careers. But its significance may be even more straightforward. One subject who participated in my research captured the connection between contentment and career development in this simple yet profound statement:

> **If I am content in my work, I have more time to focus on getting better versus getting out.**

Talented people are going to develop careers somewhere. How do you make sure it's with you and your organization? That's the question this chapter will answer. It starts with understanding, honoring, and defining what *contentment* means to individuals—and working with employees to invite more of it into their roles. You'll explore job crafting as one possible strategy, and we'll wrap up by addressing the elusive topic of work-life balance and how managers can support it.

Condone Contentment

Contentment may be a real priority for your employees—and it may be exactly what their careers need right now. But you'll know this only if they feel comfortable and safe exploring the topic with you.

Frequently considered frivolous, issues of happiness or satisfaction at work could be considered taboo by many. For people who came up through the "leave your personal life at door" ranks, addressing contentment may feel like stepping over an uncomfortable line.

As a manager, you can overcome the reluctance that your employees may experience by bringing visibility to the topic and highlighting the value of happiness to you and sharing how you prioritize your own contentment. Demonstrate what it looks like to attend to your own internal needs in this regard. Talk about its importance.

Shondra leads a team of call center supervisors for an organization that services home warranties. It's a pressure-cooker environment with high call volumes and ambitious goals related to wait times and customer satisfaction.

When Shondra took the role, she was candid with her own manager about past bouts she had suffered with stress, depression, and exhaustion, and about her commitment to maintaining happiness and balance—for herself and others. She shared her story with her team of supervisors as well, a vulnerable move for a new leader. But it paid off. Several of her employees sought her out, expressed gratitude for her vulnerability, and shared their own struggles.

Beyond building swift bonds with many team members, Shondra offered permission to others to talk about and seek out what they needed to be able to sustain their energy and enthusiasm for work. She routinely drew attention to the things she was doing for herself: walks alone at lunchtime, connecting with friends during her commute, morning meditation, taking time off as necessary to rest and rejuvenate. Sharing her experience gave her team a growing menu of ideas they could implement as well. And "How are you . . . really?" became Shondra's signature opening of one-on-ones and group meetings—and a jumping-off point for helping others consider what could bring greater contentment at work.

Prioritizing and seeking out your own contentment creates the safe and acceptable space for others to do the same. And that's the first step toward greater understanding and action.

Build Back and Build Up

Opportunities to enhance contentment spring from two different starting points that all managers should be aware of.

First, you notice something's going on with the employee. They might articulate the problem, or you might pick up on signs from their behavior—signs like low energy, disengagement, procrastination, negative emotions, and a decline in the quality of work products. These could be signals that the person is operating from a deficit of those positive emotions that support success—signals that could open the door to conversations about how to build back a level of contentment.

For instance, a manager may notice that a talented employee's performance has slipped and opens up the following dialogue.

Manager: I noticed that you're struggling with things that came easily to you before. I'd like to understand what's going on. Is this a good time?

Employee: Sure. What do you mean?

Manager: You used to crank out those reconciliations without breathing hard. Yet, over the past couple of weeks it seems more challenging. They're arriving later and with errors these days. Is there anything going on—anything I can do?

Employee: Yeah. And I'm really sorry about that. It's been a rough patch. My husband's uncle passed away and we're trying to sort out care for his disabled son. Every spare moment is over there or on the phone with possible facilities. I thought I was holding it together better than that. I guess I'm spread so thin, I'm not doing anything well.

This deeper understanding offers the manager a chance to collaborate with the employee to address the situation, prevent burnout, and take possible steps to help them move toward a greater sense of contentment.

Alternatively, things might be going well, and the employee is feeling comfortable and fine, but something is still missing. You have an opportunity to take their contentment from just good to great—and in so doing, enhance their engagement.

> Don't wait for an exit interview to learn what would
> have enhanced an employee's experience.

Build into your coaching cadence an ongoing thread of dialogue about what will bring greater satisfaction, gratification, fun, and joy into people's work. The simple act of asking will distinguish you from most managers. And when you collaborate with others to transform their responses to reality, you'll build unbeatable relationships that lead to retention and results.

Facilitate Awareness of Contentment

Contentment is highly personal, subjective, and fluid. What makes me happy is likely very different from what makes you happy. And what made me happy last year may no longer have the same effect.

> One size doesn't fit all—or even one—forever.

The desires, needs, hopes, and fears that make up our inner landscape are always in motion, changing the importance and sources of contentment over time. Yet, despite the constant roiling in our psyches, few people give serious thought to what contentment means to them. They just know that it's missing or that they need more of it. And this represents a rich opportunity for you, as a manager, to engage with others on a deep and meaningful level—one that can build trust and forge a path to a more satisfying work experience.

During my 20-plus years of leadership consulting, I've spoken with thousands of managers and employees about this subject. And while no two people have shared exactly the same thoughts, these are the most frequently cited intrinsic factors that drive an overall sense of contentment in the workplace.

You can use the following checklist of intrinsic factors that contribute to contentment in a couple of ways.

TOOL What Could Make You More Content?

- ❑ Ability to achieve and succeed
- ❑ Appreciation and recognition
- ❑ Being able to bring one's authentic self to work
- ❑ Civility in the workplace
- ❑ Development opportunities
- ❑ Empowerment and autonomy
- ❑ Flexibility
- ❑ Friendships
- ❑ Fun
- ❑ Inclusivity
- ❑ Job fit
- ❑ Meaning/meaningful work
- ❑ Nature of the work and daily activities
- ❑ Opportunities for creativity and innovation
- ❑ Positive view of the future
- ❑ Pride
- ❑ Progress
- ❑ Quality communication
- ❑ Relationship with supervisor
- ❑ Relationships with co-workers
- ❑ Resources needed for success
- ❑ Respectful, fair treatment
- ❑ Trust
- ❑ Use of talents and skills
- ❑ Variety
- ❑ Work-life balance

Consider previewing what you'll preach by using it yourself. Your understanding and actions will model the contentment you want to help others develop—and that's a huge part of condoning it. Review the list and think about what might bring you greater happiness, satisfaction, or ease at work. Check the items you'd like more of, then go back and circle the ones that are top priorities today. Develop a plan for bringing more of those priorities into your work.

Once you've worked it through for yourself, try it out with your employees in the same way. (Sometimes it's helpful to start with those with whom you already enjoy a solid and trusting relationship; this gives you a chance to try something new under less uncomfortable circumstances first.) Because thinking about what makes one happy might be new to people, give them time for reflection—maybe even inviting them to discuss it with others who know them well and might have ideas. Then, come together to explore the priorities. Strive to understand their motivations and needs. This will put you in a good position to work with the employee to identify concrete next steps for activating priority factors.

Here's the beauty of nearly all the factors on this checklist: you and the employee are able to create a plan to positively affect them. As a manager, you have a certain degree of latitude to make changes within your department or team and to individual roles—changes that can introduce greater ease, enhance enjoyment, and facilitate the kind of balance that allows people to keep going and growing. And it all begins with awareness—the employee's and yours.

WHEN YOU CAN'T SAY YES

You may feel anxious about delving into a conversation with employees about what would improve their experience and bring greater contentment to them and their jobs. If so, you're not alone. Many managers resist such exchanges—generally not because they're disinterested; rather, they just don't know how to navigate the situation when they can't say yes.

You may have no control when it comes to compensation and other factors, such as working hours, quotas, specific processes and standards, and so on. And when employees indicate an interest in these things, it's important to be truthful and transparent. A clear no today is generally more palatable than a murky maybe that dissolves into delayed disappointment tomorrow. Candor builds trust, and trust is one of the things that employees crave most.

But working with others toward greater happiness and satisfaction could uncover multiple paths that lead there. So, don't allow a no to one factor to become a roadblock. Instead, use it as an opportunity to explore the unique and multifaceted contours of what contentment means to the individual and jointly create another way to a yes.

Get (Job) Crafty

In most organizations, the one thing that managers have the greatest control over is the jobs that their people do. You can take full advantage of this as a way to introduce greater contentment into individual roles as you facilitate meaningful growth and career development. And you can do this through job crafting.

Job crafting boils down to shaping the work—what an employee does—to better meet the intrinsic needs contained in the previous checklist. Sometimes people would welcome the opportunity to:

- ▶ Do more of one thing.
- ▶ Do less of another thing.
- ▶ Do something different.
- ▶ Do it with different people.
- ▶ Activate a signature strength.
- ▶ Dip into unfamiliar waters.

As a manager, it's likely well within your purview to help make this happen by customizing the role, tasks, and responsibilities to be more appealing and aligned with what will result in greater contentment—as long as you meet your team or departmental objectives.

Work is a puzzle. Rearrange the pieces.

You likely shuffle work around on a regular basis, looking at various ways to deliver the outcomes you're responsible for with the people on your team. Well, what about doing the same thing—but with development in the foreground? That's what job crafting is all about. It's about embracing flexibility around how the work gets done so you can better meet the unique contentment needs of individual employees.

When you job craft, you can slice and dice job descriptions, reconfiguring them in ways that offer employees a better fit, more desirable activities, and greater opportunities for growth and development. It's a matter of shifting tasks among employees to introduce the variety, interest, or meaning they crave.

I learned about the power and possibilities associated with this during my first job, teaching modeling and charm classes to children through a retail chain. It didn't take me long before the program was running smoothly, and I began to feel that I needed something more to remain interested and content. My manager, Mr. K, a keen observer of his team and, seeming to sense what was going on, dropped by the studio to check in on me and my current level of engagement and fulfillment.

Because of our relationship, I felt completely comfortable sharing that things were feeling stale. He knew I was studying marketing and interested in special-events management, so we brainstormed a few ideas in that area for adding some interest to my role. Together we arrived at the perfect plan: I would wrap additional storewide special events around the seasonal fashion shows I was already producing.

These events—if they were conducted at all—were typically handled by department managers, one of the most overburdened roles in a retail store. I was delighted to have my job enriched in such a meaningful way. The department managers were delighted when Mr. K offered to have me take that responsibility off their hands. Store management was delighted to have this work done regularly, enthusiastically, and at no additional cost. And the customers were delighted with the special events that followed.

I stayed in that job (loving it and growing from it) for several more years specifically because of my manager's willingness to understand my motivation, rethink my needs, and recraft my role in a way that was beneficial all the way around.

Why be constrained by limiting and potentially less satisfying job configurations when you can mix and match elements to generate more appealing roles that deliver greater contentment? Who cares where the individual pieces of the puzzle come from as long as the final picture matches the box top—especially if that picture looks even better because it's infused with engagement and growth?

PRO TIP

Look for win-win opportunities. In retrospect, Mr. K (in the previous example) had it easy. I was eager to take on something that others were eager to shed, which made for a tidy shift. But it doesn't always work out so neatly. You can't enrich one employee's job or experience at the expense of another's. That's why ongoing dialogue with all employees is key. It's the only way you'll know your people: what they love, hate, or want more or less of. Your conversations create a repository of information that you can draw upon to meet multiple needs when opportunities arise. Because one employee's drudgery is frequently another's development.

Promote Progress

Just as rest is routinely overlooked as a contentment driver, progress frequently fails to get the attention it's due. According to researchers and authors Teresa Amabile and Steven Kramer, progress is among the most motivating factors in the workplace.[25]

Think back to some of your most frustrating, least satisfying days. They were likely punctuated with "one step forward and two steps back" moments, feelings of treading water and not getting traction, and the inability to establish momentum toward your goals. When you consider some of your best days, they're likely the ones where you were making things happen and moving things forward. Progress makes the difference.

As a manager, you're in a powerful position to help others achieve and perceive that sense of progress, which inspires and engages employees.

> **People must not only achieve—**
> **but also perceive—progress.**

The daily challenges and obstacles employees face can easily thwart feelings of progress and the contentment that accompanies them. But, as a manager, you can help by anticipating and communicating about possible problems ahead. Collaborate with others to get out in front of issues. Work to proactively clear the path by removing roadblocks. Facilitate the resources (time, budget, people) necessary so that projects and initiatives can continue to move forward.

Sometimes even when progress is being made, your employees may not see it. Incremental steps become invisible. And the daily grind can blind us to advances. You can point it out. Draw attention to the progress being made. Celebrate it. Recognize it. Encourage it.

Marco is a manager in the engineering department of a client that manufactures automotive components. He was recently promoted from being an individual contributor engineer and decided to make just one change to the weekly status update meetings. Before addressing the challenges facing each team (which was the purpose of getting together and the big agenda item), he decided to invite each attendee to share one minute of "good news." This was a time to highlight their wins, their successes, and what they've learned that's fueling their progress. For years, he had attended meetings that were mired in problems, and he wanted to shift the culture.

Marco anticipated the slow start—and even the eye rolling on the part of some engineers—but he endured the discomfort and stuck to his vision. Pretty soon, he began to notice results. He sensed more genuine enthusiasm in the "good news" reports. His team demonstrated more pride in their work. And the rest of the meeting felt less draining because the team brought more curiosity, creativity, and innovation to their problem-solving efforts.

Helping people achieve—and even just perceive—progress is a powerful and budget-neutral way to fuel greater contentment and support results as well.

Work and Life: The Eternal Balancing Act

The pandemic and its economic and employment fallout added to the already growing number of employees who were rethinking their relationship with work and their broader life priorities. More and more people find themselves adopting John Wooden's quote: "Do not let making a living prevent you from making a life."

Increasingly, "making a living" or the *work* part of the work-life balance equation is where many employees are choosing to pull back. And it makes sense when you consider that 41 percent of employees feel burned out from work, and 87 percent feel that their jobs affect their mental health.[26]

Some time ago, I began pushing back on the term *balance* to describe this delicate dance we engage in with work and our broader lives. It reminds me of multitasking. We now know that we can't actually do two things at one time; we just switch tasks quickly (and in a way that's mentally exhausting). The same holds true of work-life balance. We're generally either doing work or doing life. Switching back and forth quickly isn't balance; it's just exhausting too.

So, rather than aspiring to an elusive balance, perhaps the best we can do is help employees intentionally manage the mix of work and life in a way that offers the overall experience of contentment they're looking for.

It's impossible for people to leave their personal lives at the door when they come to work. Or to leave their work lives at the door when they come home (especially with so many working remotely from their homes). As a result, your coaching efforts can no longer focus exclusively upon professional issues; the personal ones are too intertwined, especially when it comes to navigating the messy mix that is work and life.

Success in this expanded coaching role demands more of managers. More listening. More creativity and problem solving. More support. Done well, it delivers a lot more as well. More trust. More contentment. More retention.

Helping employees consider how they might manage the mix of work and their broader lives differently may be new terrain for many managers. When the opportunity presents itself, consider asking your employees these questions to guide a rich and thoughtful conversation:

- ▶ What factors are contributing to an unsatisfactory imbalance?
- ▶ What's the danger of staying on this current path? (Consider yourself, family, friends, work.)
- ▶ What are today's most pressing (and real) priorities?
- ▶ How do today's priorities align with your larger life purpose or goals?
- ▶ What can change?

From this conversation, maybe you determine with the employee that they need to take some time off. Or you decide to shift or share responsibilities differently for a period of time. Or you provide them with access to more or different resources, such as administrative backup, flexible work schedules, coaching, and training.

The options will differ based upon the individual and the organization. Just as with job crafting, you'll want to look for win-win ways forward so that one employee's solution doesn't become another's problem. The reality is that you may not always be able to arrive at the perfect plan. But the effort you invest speaks volumes about your commitment to the employee, their effectiveness, and their career. And don't underestimate that feeling of being cared for, valued, and heard, which can alone enhance contentment.

These questions can drive conversations that surface real, raw emotions. These conversations can feel intimate. You may not have earned the right to go there at this point in your relationship. If that's the case, you can still be helpful by offering the questions for the employee's individual use. They could privately reflect upon them or dialogue with others. Making yourself and the questions available can only advance your relationship in a positive direction.

It's not your job to be a therapist. But offering this sort of thinking partnership and support is increasingly necessary to help today's employees bring their best to their work, to co-create the level of contentment they're looking for, and even to retain good talent.

PRO TIP

Know your limits. Should the work-life mix issues raised by employees exceed your capacity, call for reinforcements. Your human resources function and employee assistance program professionals would be ideal next-level resources.

The Final Word

Contentment is yet another dimension of one's career that employees can grow and expand over time. Helping others enhance their well-being, happiness, engagement, enjoyment, and balance at work is good for individuals and for business. It's squishy, uncharted territory for many. So, as a manager, you may have to help people navigate this terrain. Demonstrate that contentment is a legitimate and valued workplace need and help others think through what it means to them.

Start by identifying what employees want to experience more of. Once you've clarified that, there are likely many ways forward. Consider options such as structural adjustments (like job crafting) and a more human focus on things like support for managing the work-life mix.

"Contentment is the only real wealth."

Alfred Bernhard Nobel, a Swedish chemist, engineer, inventor,
businessman, and philanthropist with 355 patents

At the end of the day, happiness, satisfaction, balance, and ease are the metrics that matter most to employees (and to successful managers and organizations that facilitate contentment). How prepared are you to help them meet these metrics?

8

Choice

How can you help people make meaningful choices, exercise greater control over themselves, make decisions related to their work, and enjoy levels of autonomy, independence, and flexibility that support the business while encouraging them to develop and thrive?

"You're not the boss of me" is a sentiment that we've all likely felt at some time or another. That deep yearning to exercise control. To sit squarely in the driver's seat of our lives. To decide and act based upon the direction we set.

Autonomy is a fundamental psychological need that we all share. Classic research into human motivation conducted by Richard M. Ryan and Edward L. Deci in the 1970s and popularized more recently by authors like Daniel Pink in *Drive* and Susan Fowler in *Master Your Motivation* all highlight the important relationship between control and intrinsic motivation.[27] Simply put, when employees experience choice, they become more internally motivated and engaged.

However, the idea of employees experiencing greater autonomy causes a very different experience for many managers: anxiety. It's easy to think in "either-or" terms: *If they've got control, then I've lost it.* However, the idea of choice is more nuanced than that.

In my own research, employees who prioritized choice shared their thinking in words like *control* and *autonomy*. But they also used terms like *flexibility, freedom, independence,* and *options.* They expressed a desire to have influence "over the work," "freedom to decide" things related to "getting their jobs done," and the "ability to make my own choices." One respondent offered this compelling description of choice as wanting to "apply my skills and expertise in ways I feel are most effective." It's hard to not get on board with that.

In the workplace, there will always be decisions that leadership must make. What strategy to undertake, what markets to enter, and what standards to apply represent the "what" of work—and may not be up for debate. But there's a lot that managers may control unnecessarily, such as how the work gets done, where, and when. While these things have traditionally been dictated to employees, they offer rich opportunities for choice and the development and satisfaction that come along with it.

Facilitating greater autonomy isn't about allowing employees to simply do whatever they want. It's about encouraging people to bring more of themselves to work. It's about offering the opportunity for greater personal alignment and ensuring that work is a reflection of the individual. It's about enabling the authenticity that so many employees crave.

When employees enjoyed this sense of choice, they routinely reported in my research that it sent a clear signal to them—one of trust, confidence, competence, and value. Feelings of appreciation grow along with autonomy, which leads to greater engagement, contentment, performance, and retention.

The good news is that if you're putting the previous chapters and dimensions into practice with your employees, you're moving in the right direction. Choice undergirds all of the other Cs. As you explore the dimensions with employees and encourage them to prioritize which matter most, they're exercising choice. As you facilitate a planning process that has them taking the lead on next steps, you're empowering them to choose.

Choice is the foundation of the multidimensional career approach to development. At the same time, it's a discrete dimension that's important to many employees. So, here are some focused strategies for putting greater intentional emphasis on choice—and helping people grow in the process.

WHICH WOULD YOU RATHER?

Given a choice, which would you rather? Have control over others or autonomy over yourself? Studies suggest that our attraction to power is rooted in the fundamental human need for autonomy. Researchers have concluded that "people desire power not to be a master over others, but to be master of their own domain, to control their own fate."[28]

The implications of this eye-opening finding are enormous. Think about it. How many employees have mistakenly chased corporate power and promotions when what they were really looking for was the autonomy that came along with it?

This insight is a game changer for managers who struggle to keep employees growing and engaged (and who struggle to just keep employees) in an environment in which promotions aren't plentiful. It opens the door to a whole new conversation aimed at uncovering the choice-points or freedoms you might be able to say yes to—even if you must say no to the promotion itself.

To uncover the "why" behind an employee's promotion focus, consider posing questions like:

- What exactly is it about the nature of the promotion that's attractive to you?
- What kinds of decisions do you look forward to making?
- What do you look forward to having control over?
- What additional freedom do you anticipate and look forward to?

Teasing out how autonomy might be fueling interest in a promotion or another position offers an opportunity to infuse additional choice into an employee's current role. And if the researchers are right (and there's no reason to believe they're not) when they say, "Gaining autonomy quenches the desire for power," then you'll be able to build the essence of what employees want most right within their current roles.

Spotlight Forgotten Choices

Employees generally have a lot more control than they realize. Yet, as with so many things, it's easy to overlook what we become accustomed to. The freedom and flexibility that might have felt welcome and refreshing in the beginning is now taken for granted in the swirl of work. It becomes just how things are.

A new device's computing speed is noticeable for a few hours before it becomes an invisible expectation. Same with employees and choice.

As a result, it's frequently not necessary to actually elevate an employee's level of autonomy. Rather, you as their manager can authentically elevate the experience and feeling of autonomy by reacquainting people with the control they already possess.

Antoine is a bell staff team member at a luxury hotel. His manager, Leslie, made note of a couple of difficult conversations with Antoine recently during which he lamented being at the "bottom of the food chain" and at everyone else's disposal. He wanted more choice in and control over his work. As they considered the somewhat limited possibilities given the nature of his role, something important occurred to Leslie.

Because of the corporation's commitment to the customer experience, Antoine was empowered to take care of any guest concern up $500 with no approval required. Without discounting his current feelings, she reminded him of this pretty extraordinary power and asked how he was using it. He talked about how impressed he had been in the beginning—and how his friends at other companies didn't have similar authority. He also admitted that he hadn't thought much about it or used it recently.

Leslie inquired if looking for opportunities to strategically use this power might shift how Antoine felt about his role, and he was open to exploring it. So, they discussed the hotel's new service initiative and brainstormed specific ways he could use his authority to address common challenges and delight customers in the process.

A conversation like this requires finesse and nuance. It would be easy for employees to walk away feeling diminished or scolded with a message of how good they already have it. But approached with care and a sincere desire to support the employee, you can help some people recognize and revisit the autonomy that already exists within their current roles with a simple question like, "What choices or control do you exercise today?"

The conversation may take longer than you expect (because of the number of forgotten choices waiting to be unearthed). And you might be surprised at how a renewed, refreshed awareness is sometimes all that's necessary to inspire a renewed, refreshed appreciation for just how empowered somebody already is.

Pursue Choice-Points

Frequently, a reminder from you will get people in touch with the autonomy they already enjoy. Other times, they'll be ready to enjoy more. This is when you and the employee can explore additional areas where greater independence might be possible.

> Brady manages a team of consultants responsible for helping different parts of the organization manage large-scale change efforts. Jennifer has been a consultant on his team for several years and is a heavily requested resource by departments where she's consulted before. After completing the Multidimensional Career Self-Assessment, Jennifer asked to talk with him about her interest in choice.
>
> Brady spent some time reflecting on how he could offer her greater control—within the very real limitations of the job. His isn't one of those organizations that allows for flexible schedules and working from home. The methodology they use is the methodology that had to be used. And the technology for tracking and reporting is the technology that has to be used.
>
> But a couple of possibilities began bubbling up for Brady. Within their standard methodology, there was some room to flex and incorporate new approaches. And maybe it was time to allow Jennifer to select her own contractor resources rather than assigning them. With these thoughts in mind, he scheduled a time to debrief Jennifer's self-assessment and explore her interest in choice.

Expanding and developing choice can be vexing. Your organization has processes and guardrails in place for a reason. Even so, looking at things from a different perspective with curiosity and creativity may unearth opportunities. It can be helpful to deconstruct the employee's role to determine aspects of the work that might represent choice-points. While each role and organization will be unique, the Choice Points to Consider tool provides a starter list.

TOOL **Choice Points to Consider**

❑ **Tasks:** Input on how to select the actual tasks and responsibilities to be undertaken
❑ **Priorities:** Ability to determine what's most important or urgent and act accordingly
❑ **Location:** Flexibility to choose where work gets done—home, office, or elsewhere
❑ **Schedule/timing:** Freedom to conduct business on a schedule of the employee's choosing
❑ **Conditions:** Power to decide whether to work independently or with others
❑ **Team/others:** Authority to choose with whom to work
❑ **Approach:** Freedom to determine how to approach and complete the work
❑ **Sequencing:** Flexibility to switch up the order of actions
❑ **Technology:** Choice of tools that best support the employee and the work
❑ **Boundaries:** Ability to set appropriate limits and say no as appropriate
❑ **Learning opportunities:** Input on how to incorporate development experiences and skill building into the role
❑ **Other:**

Start by going through this thought process yourself and clarifying what's possible and what's not (as Brady did in the example above). Then you're ready for a conversation with the employee. Use this starter list and other aspects of the job that you've identified, reviewing each item and exploring which of the viable options are most interesting—and which might offer the greatest growth.

Then make a plan for them to take on greater choice. Keep in mind that most employees will benefit from a controlled transition. They may need additional training. Or a deeper understanding of the big picture so they can make aligned decisions. Or access to new systems or processes. Or familiarity with upstream and downstream work processes so they can remain a vital link. Anticipate and plan for the support that will be required, knowing that your investment now will be returned with greater autonomy, confidence, and self-sufficiency in the future.

During Brady's conversation with Jennifer, he was candid about the dimensions of the role that were off-limits, like scheduling and location. But she got excited when he mentioned the possibility of augmenting the standard approach with some new tools. She'd read a lot about how other organizations were using text-based learning to support enterprise-wide change and build new habits. She really wanted to begin experimenting with this technology, and she already had an internal client in mind. This could offer her an opportunity to learn more about an emerging field.

And the prospect of selecting her own resources was interesting as well. Jennifer liked the idea of building her own team and could immediately see how learning to interview and hire contractors would enhance her leadership capacity and prepare her for broader responsibilities in the future. So, Brady and Jennifer dug into co-creating a plan to ensure that she had the time and got the training she needed to exercise this new level of choice successfully.

PRO TIP

Beware the paradox of choice. Strive to strike the right balance between too many options (which can be stressful, overwhelming, and even debilitating) and too few. Turning over control of one or possibly two choice-points is generally enough to offer a different experience, facilitate new insights and growth, and generate a sense of satisfaction. More than that and you may miss the sweet spot—and sour the experience for the employee, the organization, and yourself.

Become a Macromanager

Micromanager: it's one of the least flattering labels in business today. It paints the picture of an intrusive level of involvement in the work and work products. Nitpickiness and attention to unnecessary details. An excessive need for control that produces an unpleasant and unproductive environment.

Fortunately, the alternative can deliver better business outcomes in a way that allows employees to grow and thrive: macromanagement! It's an approach to dealing with employees and others in a way that honors who they are and what they know, along with their innate need for choice and autonomy.

Whereas micromanagement is the enemy of choice, macromanagement is its champion. Macromanagers offer the structure people need without smothering them. They create the space for employees to step up in new ways. And they inspire innovation, ownership, and engagement.

Where do you stand? Are you a little more micro or macro in your approach to managing others? Use the Are You a Micro- or Macromanager tool on the next page to consider your natural tendencies. Just mark where along each continuum you honestly fall. There's no right or wrong—just be real.

In reality, all managers have a bit of both approaches within them. (And if you're anything like I am, I'll bet the micromanager part is a lot more pronounced during times of stress and overwhelm.) But effective, self-aware leaders understand their natural dispositions, consciously flexing and moving toward the right side of the scale to meet the needs of employees—especially those looking for greater choice.

Macromanagers get out of the weeds— and out of the way of employees.

If you'd like to migrate in the direction of macromanagement—and be able to offer greater choice to employees—there are a few things you can do.

> ▶ **Internalize the big picture.** Micromanagement is frequently the result of focusing on the weeds because you don't know or aren't familiar enough with the 10,000-foot view. It's no wonder some managers become hyper-attentive to those things they have control over, demand to be kept in the loop on routine matters, and obsess over insignificant details. The antidote is to helicopter up. Explore and really understand the big picture. Do your own research into organizational priorities, strategies, and tactics. Talk with colleagues in other departments. Ask your own manager to share what they know about future direction and plans. Understanding where the business is headed creates the guardrails for success. This allows for more creativity, flexibility, and freedom in terms of how employees get there.

Micromanagers focus on:	Macromanagers focus on:

How
I tend to define and dictate the process or methods associated with accomplishing a task.

What
I tend to clarify the goals and requirements of the end product or what's to be delivered.

◄─────────────────────────►

Directives
It's my way to give instructions and marching orders.

Directions
It's my way to establish the destination and let them figure out how to get there.

◄─────────────────────────►

Compliance
My superpower is ensuring that processes have been followed and results delivered precisely as outlined.

Commitment
My superpower is tapping engagement to ensure a sustainable source of energy, ideas, and deep connection to the organization's mission.

◄─────────────────────────►

Coordination
I'm at my best when acting as a conductor at the hub of the wheel, accepting and funneling information where it's required.

Collaboration
I'm at my best when I'm encouraging connections among group or team members to ensure strong bonds and ongoing networking to serve individuals and the organization as a whole

◄─────────────────────────►

Monitoring
I serve others by staying on top of the project plan, routinely checking the details, ferociously following up, and ensuring that commitments are delivered.

Mentoring
I serve others by helping them build the capacity to self-check and deliver results in a way that helps them grow and become more autonomous.

◄─────────────────────────►

- ▶ **Lead with versatility.** Micromanagement is in the eye of the beholder . . . or the person being managed. New, complex tasks absolutely demand expert advice, guidance, and detailed direction. Anything less would be setting your employees (and likely your customers and stakeholders) up for failure. But in cases where the employee is experienced and proficient, there's likely room to adopt a more macro approach that will allow for greater control and choice. Assess the level of employee competence and confidence as a basis for determining how much latitude will offer the desired autonomy while also ensuring necessary business outcomes.
- ▶ **Monitor what matters.** As you expand choice, transfer control, and allow greater freedom over how employees approach work, watch the metrics and indicators that most closely align with success. If the important measures are moving in the right direction—if your team is delivering what's required—then you've found the appropriate level of control and independence. Faltering results, however, offer an opportunity to revisit the level of autonomy, determine if changes are required, and help redirect employees toward more effective effort and choices.

At its core, macromanagement is a development strategy that allows you to position others to learn more, do more, and be more. It's also a powerful way to think about offering more choice and enabling employees to enjoy the autonomy they need to grow and thrive.

Expand and Enable Decision Making

In many ways, choice boils down to the extent to which people are allowed to make decisions. Greater decision-making authority and the opportunity to decide issues with greater complexity and stakes represent meaningful ways to enhance an employee's sense of autonomy—and to enable new growth opportunities in the process.

Avoid the Parenting 101 trap. As a young mother, I learned to build my children's sense of autonomy (and minimize the angst of getting them dressed in the morning) by letting them make decisions. Grey pants or blue pants? Ponytail or headband? Tall socks or short socks? Things didn't always match, but we got the job done. *Don't try this with employees!* They aren't children. And they can see these kinds of cosmetic choice-points a mile away.

The question managers must ask themselves is this: Which decisions can you give or delegate to others?

Tom is the executive director of a regional nonprofit, and Reina is a fundraising/development associate who's been in the role for about 18 months. Reina learned the job quickly and has been performing well. Understanding that they are a bare-bones team with few opportunities to change roles or even responsibilities, she decided that she wanted her next growth opportunity to come through exercising greater choice. And she asked to schedule a chat with Tom.

Tom spent some time preparing for the meeting, considering Reina's current level of knowledge and skill and her readiness for less direction. He also contemplated both the decisions he could share with others and those that Reina was prepared to begin making and identified a particularly relevant one.

When Tom met with Reina, he suggested that she take responsibility for determining which donors would be advanced to the personal outreach tier. Her success required an understanding of the organization's mission, historical giving patterns, and donor psychographics, all things that Tom had handled previously. But he knew that Reina had the grounding to make the right decision at least 90 percent of the time. And she was thrilled with the additional responsibility and freedom to make such important decisions.

The decisions that you make on a daily basis may be routine to you, but they are rich opportunities for those around you. They are opportunities for trial and error. Experimentation and mistakes. Learning and improvement.

Choices Have Consequences

As instructive as making decisions and exercising choice can be, the most profound learning comes as your employees develop the capacity to own and address the consequences of those decisions. Greater choice ups the ante and offers a crash course in accountability in new, bigger, and sometimes more visible ways.

**Owning a decision means owning the
success or failure associated with it.**

Handing off decisions is an important first step toward enhancing choice and greater control over an employee's role. But it's just the first—and maybe the easiest. Effective managers understand that taking a "delegate a decision and dash" approach won't deliver results to the business, or development to employees. Success depends largely upon the ongoing support you provide.

This includes checking in with employees. Recognizing their efforts. Tracking the decisions they're making. Providing recognition and feedback. Offering the coaching they may need as they assume greater decision-making responsibility.

The key word in that last sentence is *coaching*. Not oversharing advice or setting the direction or dictating next steps. Coaching. That's because the only way for people to become competent and confident in making decisions is to make decisions. Coaching means overcoming what may be your "helpful" and "efficient" knee-jerk reaction of just telling them what to do.

The problem with that approach is that it's not helpful. And in the long run, it's not efficient either. Instead, effective managers coach emerging decision-making skills with thought-provoking questions. The Coaching for Expanded Decision Making worksheet on the next page offers a framework or agenda that you can use with employees to facilitate conversations designed to build and expand decision making in a supportive way.

TOOL Coaching for Expanded Decision Making

1. What are you trying to accomplish/achieve/solve?

2. What's at stake? What are the consequences of the decision?

3. What information have you gathered/considered?

4. What actions have you considered?

5. What are the merits and downsides of each alternative?

6. How do the alternatives align with our mission, values, and standards?

7. How do the alternatives affect the customer?

8. What's the worst-case scenario?

9. Who else have you consulted?

10. Who else might you consult?

11. What's your next step?

A coaching mindset and questions like these create the space for dialogue. They carve out a pause for reflection. They help to bring order to the ideas that are swirling around in the employee's mind. They allow people to test and refine their thinking. And they offer a structure that, over time, employees will internalize and be able to apply independently, which inspires an upward spiral of autonomy and choice.

The Final Word

Choice is a fundamental psychological need that employees bring to the workplace. Whether it takes the form of more autonomy, flexibility, or greater decision making, it's a powerful motivator and force for growth. While there will always be plenty of strategies, policies, and organizational directives that are out of your hands, there are also plenty of meaningful decisions about how these things are implemented that you can share with employees. And when you do that, you offer the opportunity for them to grow their ownership, alignment, engagement, and capacity.

Start by helping people recognize the autonomy they already have and might be taking for granted. Work with them to tease out additional choices that are available. As you trade micromanagement for macromanagement, you'll share more control, enable greater decision making, and facilitate the growth that comes from owning the outcomes of decisions one makes—both good and bad.

"Choices are the hinges of destiny."

Edwin Markham, 20th century poet

They are likely the hinges of careers as well. How can you keep those hinges well-oiled so that employees can walk through the door of opportunity?

9

Possibilities Are the New Promotion

For decades, promotions have been the default definition of career development, establishing unattainable and unsustainable expectations for millions of employees who didn't know there was another way to grow. The fallout of this can be seen all around you. In engagement results. Organizational culture surveys. Unwanted turnover.

But employees aren't the only ones who've been victimized by this narrow and outdated definition. So have you. And so has every other manager who's tried valiantly to work within and around this broken system: Every manager who's ever been criticized or poorly rated by an employee who's been conditioned to want what's available to only a few. Every manager who's ever avoided engaging in career conversations just to minimize the potential disappointment and conflict. Every manager who's ever lost sleep at the prospect of top talent leaving over a title.

The problem was never you or your employees alone. The problem is that promotions are a small part of what makes up careers and career development. For too long, we've zoomed in and focused exclusively on that tiny part of the landscape, which has blinded us to other, more accessible dimensions that will allow employees to grow and thrive at any point throughout their careers.

From Promotions to Possibilities

It's time to broaden the definition of *career*, *career development*, and *career success* to include the additional seven dimensions that are even more interesting to employees than the traditional climb. Doing so immediately creates a wide-open playing field for growth. This expanded definition illuminates the vast opportunities that fall well within a manager's control—opportunities for development independent of positions, titles, promotions, pathways, or any other organizationally regulated and restricted artifact.

> **Taking a career to the next level doesn't have to mean moving to the next level.**

The dimensions offer a new lens with a broader focus and a way to help people explore greater:

- ▸ **Contribution** by satisfying their desire to make a difference—whether by doing more, adding value, taking greater ownership, being of service, or aligning with one's purpose.
- ▸ **Competence** by allowing them to intentionally develop the skills, knowledge, and capabilities they need to enjoy greater effectiveness, influence, and satisfaction today while ensuring continued relevance tomorrow.
- ▸ **Connection** by supporting the steps necessary to expand and deepen their social networks, build productive relationships, cultivate a sense of community, and enjoy greater visibility.
- ▸ **Confidence** by cultivating a realistic understanding of and authentic appreciation for where both their abilities and limitations lie.
- ▸ **Challenge** by allowing them to step up, step out, and step into situations that help them stretch beyond what's known and explore new, different, and difficult experiences.
- ▸ **Contentment** by helping them find within their current roles the heightened sense of satisfaction, pleasure, and ease they may need or desire.

▶ **Choice** by enabling them to exercise greater control over themselves, make decisions related to their work, and enjoy more autonomy, independence, and flexibility.

And, speaking of control, these seven dimensions are within yours! No approvals required. No budget authorization. No limitations or restrictions on the number of people who are allowed to develop. Development like this is within your domain and at your discretion and creates possibilities far beyond what promotions can offer.

Won't People Still Want Promotions?

When I talk with managers about this multidimensional approach to career development, I'm often asked, "Won't people still want promotion?" And my answer is, "Of course."

Although I'd like to think that our obsession with promotions will become passé, the truth is that employee interest in climbing the corporate ladder will persist—at least for some, for a while—until a few things shift. Until we stop training children to associate work with fixed positions by asking what they want to *be* when they grow up and help them think about work in terms of what they want to *do*. Until we move beyond societal pressure to respond to "What do you do for a living?" with labels and titles. Until cultural and generational expectations linking the velocity of our movement to our value fade. And until organizations come to terms with and innovate their approaches to compensation and perks so that money doesn't become a driving motivation for movement.

It will take some time to replace something that's so deeply embedded in our structures and psyches. As a manager, you're on the front lines of this battle. And your actions have the power to start chipping away yesterday's thinking. The research is clear: Employees are more interested in developing through contribution, competence, connection, confidence, challenge, contentment, and choice than the climb. The possibilities associated with these alternative dimensions resonate and give them hope. Tapping into that hope is how you will effect change.

Despite your best efforts, though, you'll likely still encounter those hard-core old-schoolers. You know the ones—those who can't get past their preoccupations with positions and promotions. The ones who'll nod, smile, and say, "Thanks, that's all very nice, but how do I get to be a _____?"

Going from yesterday to today's thinking won't happen overnight. But don't worry. You have the tools to guide thinking forward. Here's what you can do.

1. Understand What's Animating Their Interest

Too frequently, managers take an employee's request for a promotion at face value. And when it's not possible to comply (which, let's face it, is most of the time), they try to gently close the door on the conversation. But in the process, they miss the opportunity to explore what's motivating the interest and identify other potential ways forward.

Instead, you can use requests and conversations about promotions as a chance to learn more. Ask questions that get behind what employees really want—and uncover important cues about alternative ways to meet their needs. Try questions like:

▶ What exactly is it about that role that interests you most?

▶ What part of it do you look forward to doing most?

▶ Which responsibilities do you believe will be the most interesting?

▶ Which responsibilities might be the most challenging?

▶ What will you need to be able to do to be highly effective in the role?

▶ Where might there be gaps between where you are today and what would be expected of you in that role?

These questions tease out the nature of the work and skills required from the role itself. They slow people down and inspire reflection, in order to think beneath the surface and beyond their habitual desires to keep moving up. And they offer you, as the manager, opportunities to meet an employee's deeper needs even in the absence of the promotion they may be seeking.

2. Be Honest About What's Possible

The only thing that disappoints people more than not getting a promotion is being strung along and manipulated, only to be denied the opportunity down the line. Employees deserve the truth. And, given today's access to information about what's available or what's possible, they're going to get it, whether from you or another source.

Does the employee lack the required education or skills? Has someone already been selected for the role? Will that role not be vacated for some time to come? Is that role likely to disappear? Be honest. No manager wants to disappoint direct reports. And these conversations are rarely comfortable. But your willingness to share a hard truth demonstrates a genuine commitment to and investment in others. This earns you the right to find alternative ways forward.

3. Position the Dimensions as a Means to Their Ends

When an employee remains committed to a promotion despite your honest assessment of what's possible (or not possible), the other dimensions offer a way to grow strategically today in preparation for something else when, as, and if it materializes in the future. For instance:

If the employee will need this to be ready for a possible future promotion . . .	Then you can explore ways they can grow this in the interim . . .
To be recognized as someone who goes above and beyond, giving more than is expected	Contribution
Specific skills and abilities they don't possess today	Competence
Exposure to key players and stakeholders in other parts of the business	Connection
The ability to speak up, challenge authority, and hold their own under challenging circumstances	Confidence
To be known as someone who's not afraid of the hard stuff and consistently delivers results	Challenge
Patience to wait it out until the desired role is available	Contentment
More independent decision-making experience and authority	Choice

While you may not be able to shake some employees loose of their commitment to promotions, you don't have to abandon this book's broader, contemporary definition of *career development.* You can simply use the seven dimensions as means to their ends. The worst thing that will happen is that they may never get promoted—but they'll grow during the process and so will your relationship. And they may even experience the satisfaction of this more expansive, organic approach to development.

It's Time to Get Started

This book will end shortly. Then the real work will begin. Integrating new ideas—especially ones that run counter to organizational tradition or culture—can feel daunting. So, let me offer four possible starting points as a way to get your creative juices flowing.

> ▶ **Start small.** You don't have to do everything at once. Simply choose one employee—maybe someone with whom you have a solid relationship and who might offer you some grace as you try out this new approach. Invite them to complete the Multidimensional Career Self-Assessment described in the resources section that follows. Schedule a short meeting to jointly review the assessment results. Suggest that you and the person go think about the development priorities and possible ways to address them. Then come back to this book and review the relevant chapters to refresh your memory and identify possible strategies. Reconvene, brainstorm ideas, and develop a plan to grow the dimensions of greatest interest. (Note: Start small so you can enjoy success, work out the kinks in a safe environment, and gain some competence with this approach, but don't stay small. As soon as you feel confident, you'll want to scale your efforts to help your entire team grow.)
>
> ▶ **Start a discussion.** Invite your whole team to complete the Multidimensional Career Self-Assessment. Then focus an upcoming meeting on the results. Encourage employees to share what they learned about themselves and their development priorities. Explore how they might support one another as you turn development into a team sport.

- ▶ **Start a movement.** Share the concepts in this book with your colleagues and other managers in your organization. Conduct a book-club-style discussion and explore how you can, as a group, socialize and implement the ideas more broadly. When more of you put this updated definition of career development into practice, it sends a clear message and can more swiftly shift the culture. (Or, at a minimum, you've got others with whom to collaborate, commiserate, and celebrate successes.)
- ▶ **Start with yourself.** The best lab for these ideas is you and your own career. Try it out for yourself. See how it feels to intentionally develop some of the dimensions that might not have been on your radar screen before. Determine which tools work best for you. Model a commitment to growing beyond promotions and positions. Run a campaign of attraction rather than promotion by sharing your personal experience with employees. Pretty soon they'll be coming to you to seek out a new way to develop.

Above all, just start. The stakes associated with perpetuating the old definition of career and career development are too high. The need for skillful, engaged, contributing employees becomes greater by the day. And continuing to confuse career development with attaining specific positions will only limit the growth that both employees and organizations need.

You now possess a new, more hopeful, and possibility-fueled approach—one that allows you to redefine career development in ways that help employees thrive throughout their careers.

Put this multidimensional approach into practice and soon you'll see needless disengagement, preventable dissatisfaction, and unnecessary turnover join promotions as so yesterday.

Acknowledgments

Who would have imagined that Lisa Spinelli-White's simple request for a couple of blog posts for the ATD website would have led to *Promotions Are So Yesterday* and the joyful journey of publishing this book? I'm deeply grateful for the opportunity to work with the remarkable professionals at ATD Press. Lisa's original invitation and enthusiastic encouragement and guidance throughout have been a gift. Jack Harlow, who read the article and envisioned this book long before anyone else, was the perfect editor, offering thoughtful and thought-provoking feedback that brought the ideas to life. Kay Hechler pulled out all the stops and supported this book in ways I never expected. Working with her and Suzy Felchlin was like a master class in marketing. Melissa Jones skillfully guided the process, bringing together the perfect resources each step of the way. This includes Caroline Coppel, who added a lovely layer of polish while copyediting, and Shirley Raybuck and Kathleen Dyson whose smart and engaging page layout contributed enormously. I'm grateful to Jamie Connelly for her gracious sales support and Emmanuel Okafor for persevering and ensuring that this book found its proper buying category. And many thanks to Rose Richey for interpreting the book's premise in her creative cover design.

But that's just part of the team behind *Promotions Are So Yesterday*. I'm fortunate to be surrounded by many talented individuals who contribute to my life and work on a daily basis. Their efforts make mine possible. I'm grateful to Brett Atkin for a decade of extraordinary digital guidance and website support, Lorianne Speaks for her friendship and ability to handle whatever comes her way—always with a smile, and LaRay Gates for consistently interpreting and enhancing my ideas through her graphical magic and for creating the images and art throughout this book. Thank you to Jennifer Kuhlman for leading my social media marketing effort so creatively and effectively, Linda Blochberger for the confidence she inspires in every document she edits, Sarah Ngu for research and literature review, and Jennifer Miller for content development and an always keen editing eye. Kudos to Susan Jensen and the Digital Ranch team for creating such a smart, user-friendly online assessment.

I couldn't have completed this book without the support of my longtime business partner and friend, Karen Voloshin. Her insights, clarity, and willingness to pick up the slack were instrumental from the start. Thank you to Mark Haines, Erin Anderson, Wally Bock, and Jodi Lovitt for their friendship and technical expertise and for helping me over the humps. And I appreciate Jennifer Berkley of The Insight Advantage for conducting the research that resulted in the multidimensional career framework, and Craig Perrin for turning it into a digestible summary of insights.

Launching and marketing a book can be a daunting task. For me, it was much easier as a result of engaging with the best minds in the business. I couldn't be more grateful to Fauzia Burke, Anna Sacca, and the FSB Associates team. Beyond offering her years of publishing experience and deep understanding of publicity and public relations, Fauzia came up with the book's title. And thank you to Becky Robinson and Weaving Influence for building on the work they did with my original book and taking this one to a new level.

Despite the remarkable support of these people and others, this book would have remained a blog had it not been for my family. Words can't express my gratitude to my husband, Peter Giulioni, for all he has done to enable my work. From reading every single word (twice!), to offering his perspective, to eating way more carryout than anyone deserves, to bolstering my spirits every time I decided I couldn't do it, to reminding me to enjoy the journey—Peter's soul and love are baked into every chapter of this book. And every parent blessed with a daughter knows the joy she can bring; mine, Jenna Giulioni, certainly brought lots of it to this process. Whether it was reading a chapter and offering sweet, insightful, and frequently laugh-out-loud funny feedback; facilitating late-night title-brainstorming sessions; generating book cover concepts; or cheering me on with her signature "Ma, you got this," Jenna was a real asset to the team. I'm blessed to have my son and daughter-in-law, Nick and Diane, on Team Giulioni as well. Both successful tech and real estate investment professionals, they still found time to offer their invaluable insights, support, and love.

While there's no way (and certainly not enough space) to list them all, I owe the clients with whom I've worked and the thousands of leaders in my workshops and webinars over the years a debt of gratitude. Their generosity and willingness to share their experiences, challenges, and best practices have enriched my life and informed my work.

And finally, a second book is possible only following a first successful effort. I am deeply grateful to Beverly Kaye for inviting me to co-author *Help Them Grow or Watch Them Go*—and for generously opening the door to the new and exhilarating opportunities that came with it.

Additional Resources

If you feel like this book is just the beginning, you're absolutely right! And that's why I'm delighted to share additional resources that will allow you to learn more, delve deeper, engage your employees in a new way of approaching career development, and maybe even influence your organization and management to do the same.

Your Multidimensional Career: A Self-Assessment

Would you like help introducing your employees to this new multidimension career framework? Invite them to complete the complimentary online assessment. In less than 20 minutes, they'll be oriented to the eight development dimensions and learn about those that interest them most. Their personalized feedback reports will explain that "promotions are so yesterday" and build the case for a more expansive definition of career development. The report will also offer reflection questions to prepare employees for a thoughtful career conversation with you.

Scan the QR code or visit PromotionsAreSoYesterday.com/assessment to access the online assessment. If you'd prefer to go low-tech, you'll find a clean copy of the paper-based assessment from chapter 1 on page 137.

Multidimensional Career Workshops and Training

Would you like the managers and employees in your organization to embrace the multidimensional career framework and use it as a tool for enhancing development, engagement, retention, and business results?

Learn more about the live and virtual learning options that are available to meet your organization's unique needs. Scan the QR code or visit PromotionsAreSoYesterday.com/training to get started.

Career Development Today: What People Really Want

Are you interested in learning more about the research behind the multidimensional career framework? Scan the QR code or visit PromotionsAreSoYesterday.com/research-report to read a summary report that offers highlights of the findings as well as information about the methodology and approach.

Your Multidimensional Career: A Self-Assessment

Circle the number that best describes your level of interest in each of the following items. Then, transfer the numbers to the table and add up the columns to arrive at totals for each development dimension. Higher numbers represent dimensions you might be most interested in developing. Lower numbers suggest less interest.

To What Extent Are You Interested In . . .	Less Interested				More Interested
1 Making significant contributions?	1	2	3	4	5
2 Learning as much as possible?	1	2	3	4	5
3 Cultivating relationships with others?	1	2	3	4	5
4 Building a sense of confidence in your abilities?	1	2	3	4	5
5 Stretching beyond your comfort zone?	1	2	3	4	5
6 Enjoying your work more?	1	2	3	4	5
7 Exercising greater control over how you do your work?	1	2	3	4	5
8 Getting promoted?	1	2	3	4	5
9 Making a difference and adding greater value?	1	2	3	4	5
10 Building specific skills or enhancing a talent?	1	2	3	4	5
11 Expanding your network?	1	2	3	4	5
12 Trusting your capacity to produce consistent, predictable results?	1	2	3	4	5
13 Exploring challenging experiences?	1	2	3	4	5
14 Feeling satisfied and fulfilled with your work?	1	2	3	4	5
15 Having more flexibility?	1	2	3	4	5
16 Changing roles or positions?	1	2	3	4	5

Your Multidimensional Career: A Self-Assessment (cont.)

To What Extent Are You Interested In . . .	Less Interested			More Interested	
17 Aligning with your purpose for greater meaning at work?	1	2	3	4	5
18 Developing deeper expertise and effectiveness?	1	2	3	4	5
19 Creating a community of resources around you?	1	2	3	4	5
20 Feeling like "you've got this" in all aspects of your work?	1	2	3	4	5
21 Taking on or trying something entirely new?	1	2	3	4	5
22 Striking the appropriate work-life balance?	1	2	3	4	5
23 Exercising greater decision-making authority?	1	2	3	4	5
24 Securing a specific title?	1	2	3	4	5

1	2	3	4	5	6	7	8
9	10	11	12	13	14	15	16
17	18	19	20	21	22	23	24
Total ___	Total ___	Total ___	Total ___	Total ___	Total ___	Total ___	Total ___
Contribution	Competence	Connection	Confidence	Challenge	Contentment	Choice	Climb

Promotions Are So Yesterday
Discussion Guide

With its focus on contemporary workplace themes and strategies managers can use to develop every employee, *Promotions Are So Yesterday* is ideal for your book club or informal conversation. After the group has read the book and taken the self-assessment on page 137, use these prompts to start the conversation. Be ready for the dialogue to go in a variety of different directions and for the group to enjoy a rich learning experience.

1. What does "career" mean to you, and has your concept of career shifted or changed over the course of your working life? If so, how?

2. Which of the eight development dimensions or Cs (contribution, competence, connection, confidence, challenge, contentment, choice, climb) is most interesting to you? Which is the least interesting? Why might that be?

3. Which of the development dimensions are easiest to act upon in your organization? Which might be more challenging to facilitate?

4. How do your employees define "career"?

5. How frequently do you find yourself engaging in career conversations? What do those conversations look like?

6. What advice from the book will help you start having conversations or help you have richer conversations with your employees?

7. Which of the development dimensions might be most interesting to your employees? Why?

8. What is one step you can take to help employees expand their definitions of career development and adopt a multidimensional career mindset?

Notes

1. HayGroup, "How to Stop Your Talent Taking Flight," HayGroup, 2015, focus. kornferry.com/wp-content/uploads/2015/02/Hay-Group-Retention-Study.pdf.

2. LinkedIn, *2021 Workplace Learning Report* (Linkedin Learning, 2021), learning. linkedin.com/resources/workplace-learning-report.

3. Instructure; Bridge, "How to Get Today's Employees to Stay and Engage? Develop Their Careers," PR Newswire News Release, June 3, 2019, prnewswire. com/news-releases/how-to-get-todays-employees-to-stay-and-engage -develop-their-careers-300860067.html.

4. Julie Winkle Giulioni and Olivia Gamber, *Workplace Priorities, Beliefs & Practices: A Generational Snapshot* (Julie Winkle Giulioni, 2016), juliewinklegiulioni.com /wp-content/uploads/2021/07/JWG-Workplace-Priorities-Beliefs-Practices -Report-.pdf.

5. Julie Winkle Giulioni, *Career Development Today: What People Really Want* (Julie Winkle Giulioni, 2021), promotionsaresoyesterday.com/research-report.

6. Robert Half Management Resources, "Majority of Workers Want More Insight on How Their Efforts Affect Bottom Line," PR Newswire Press Release, August 4, 2016, prnewswire.com/news-releases/majority-of-workers-want -more-insight-on-how-their-efforts-affect-bottom-line-300309073.html.

7. PricewaterhouseCoopers, *Upskilling: Building Confidence in an Uncertain World* (New York: PwC, 2020), pwc.com/gx/en/ceo-survey/2020/trends/pwc-talent -trends-2020.pdf.

8. Gartner, "Strategies to Address Skill Gaps," Gartner, 2019, gartner.com/en /human-resources/insights/skills-gap.

9. Institute for the Future and Dell Technologies, *The Future of Work: Forecasting Emerging Technologies' Impact on Work in the Next Era of Human-Machine Partnerships* (Palo Alto, CA: Institute for the Future for Dell Technologies, 2019), iftf.org/realizing2030-futureofwork.

10. The Editors of Encyclopaedia Britannica, "Émile Coué," Encyclopaedia Britannica Online, June 28, 2021, britannica.com/biography/Emile-Coue.

11. Rob Cross, "To Be Happier at Work, Invest More in Your Relationships," *Harvard Business Review*, July 30, 2019. hbr.org/2019/07/to-be-happier-at-work-invest-more-in-your-relationships.

12. Richard M. Ryan and Edward L. Deci, *Intrinsic Motivation and Self-Determination in Human Behavior* (New York: Plenum, 1985).

13. Katherine W. Phillips, Tracy L. Dumas, and Nancy P. Rothbard, "Diversity and Authenticity," *Harvard Business Review*, March-April 2018, hbr.org/2018/03/diversity-and-authenticity.

14. Dropbox Team, "Dropbox Goes Virtual First," Dropbox blog, October 13, 2020. blog.dropbox.com/topics/company/dropbox-goes-virtual-first.

15. Liz Lewis, "Confidence at Work: Why Employers Should Nurture This Soft Skill," Indeed Lead blog, January 23, 2020. indeed.com/lead/confidence-at-work.

16. Jasmine Aquino, "Feeling Like a Fraud?" *TD*, July 1, 2020. td.org/magazines/td-magazine/feeling-like-a-fraud.

17. Tara Sophia Mohr, "Why Women Don't Apply for Jobs Unless They're 100% Qualified," *Harvard Business Review*, August 25, 2014, hbr.org/2014/08/why-women-dont-apply-for-jobs-unless-theyre-100-qualified; Christine L. Exley and Judd B. Kessler, "The Gender Gap in Self-Promotion," National Bureau of Economic Research Working Paper, no. 26345, issued October 2019, revised May 2021, nber.org/papers/w26345; Deanne Tockey and Maria Ignatova, *Gender Insights Report: How Women Find Jobs Differently* (Sunnyvale, CA: LinkedIn Talent Insights, March 2019), business.linkedin.com/content/dam/me/business/en-us/talent-solutions-lodestone/body/pdf/Gender-Insights-Report.pdf.

18. Jack Zenger and Joseph Folkman, "Research: Women Score Higher Than Men in Most Leadership Skills," *Harvard Business Review*, June 25, 2019, hbr.org/2019/06/research-women-score-higher-than-men-in-most-leadership-skills.

19. Nadja Walter, Lucie Nikoleizig, and Dorothee Alfermann, "Effects of Self-Talk Training on Competitive Anxiety, Self-Efficacy, Volitional Skills, and

Performance: An Intervention Study With Junior Sub-elite Athletes," *Sports (Basel)* 7, no. 6 (2019): 148.

20. Nigel Davies, "'Happiness Crews' and 'Culture Committees' Are Making Isolated Workers Feel Less Lonely," *Forbes*, October 11, 2019, forbes.com /sites/nigeldavies/2019/10/11/happiness-crews-and-culture-committees -are-making-isolated-workers-feel-less-lonely/?sh=561e27201927; Carolyn Gregoire, "Google's 'Jolly Good Fellow' on the Power of Emotional Intelligence," HuffPost, September 29, 2013 (updated December 6, 2017), huffpost.com/entry/googles-jolly-good-fellow_n_3975944.

21. Andrew J. Oswald, Eugenio Proto, and Daniel Sgroi, "Happiness and Productivity," *Journal of Labor Economics* 33, no. 4 (2015): 789–822.

22. Emiliana R. Simon-Thomas, "The Four Keys to Happiness at Work," *Greater Good Magazine*, August 29, 2018, greatergood.berkeley.edu/article/item/the _four_keys_to_happiness_at_work.

23. Reeshad S. Dalal, M. Baysinger, B.J. Brummel, and J.M. LeBreton, "The Relative Importance of Employee Engagement, Other Job Attitudes, and Trait Affect as Predictors of Job Performance," *Journal of Applied Social Psychology* 42, no. S1 (2012): E295–E325.

24. Simon-Thomas, "The Four Keys to Happiness at Work."

25. Steven Kramer and Teresa Amabile, *The Progress Principle: Using Small Wins to Ignite Joy, Engagement, and Creativity at Work* (Cambridge, MA: Harvard Business Review Press, 2011).

26. Michelle Delgado and Francesca Ortegren, "Employees and Companies Are Facing a Burnout Crisis," Clever, March 15, 2021 (updated August 3, 2021), listwithclever.com/research/mental-health-2021.

27. Deci and Ryan, *Intrinsic Motivation and Self-Determination*; Daniel Pink, *Drive: The Surprising Truth About What Motivates Us* (New York: Riverhead, 2009); Susan Fowler, *Master Your Motivation: Three Scientific Truths for Achieving Your Goals* (San Francisco: Berrett-Koehler, 2019).

28. Joris Lammers, Janka I. Stoker, Floor Rink, and Adam D. Galinsky. "To Have Control Over or to Be Free From Others? The Desire for Power Reflects a Need for Autonomy," *Personality and Social Psychology Bulletin* 42, no. 4 (2016): 498–512.

Index

About the Author

Credit: Jamie Nease Portraits

Julie Winkle Giulioni is a champion for workplace growth and development. Her work is based upon the belief that everyone deserves the opportunity to reach their potential. And for 30 years, she's been supporting organizations and leaders who want to make that happen with training, consulting, and keynote speeches.

Blending her background in academia as a university professor and department chair with deep industry and consulting expertise, Julie offers a pragmatic, practical, and performance-enhancing approach to leadership and career development. She's a regular columnist for *Training Industry* magazine and *SmartBrief*, and contributes articles on a range of workplace topics and trends to publications such as the *Economist*.

Named by *Inc.* magazine as a Top 100 Leadership Speaker, Julie offers in-person and virtual training and keynote presentations that offer fresh, inspiring, and actionable strategies for leaders who are interested in both their own growth and supporting the growth of others.

Julie's first book, *Help Them Grow or Watch Them Go: Career Conversations Organizations Need and Employees Want*, was an international bestseller and has been translated into six languages.

Julie is the proud mom of a daughter who's pursuing a doctorate in physical therapy, and a son and daughter-in-law who are both tech and real estate investment professionals. She lives in a 100-plus-year-old home in South Pasadena, California, with her exceedingly patient husband and their sweet rescue pooch, Pixel.

You can keep up with Julie through her website (JulieWinkleGiulioni.com), blog, LinkedIn, Twitter, and YouTube channel.